W. H. Griffith Thomas, D. D.

W. H. Griffith Thomas is known throughout the Anglo-Saxon world as one of the great English divines of modern times. From the principalship of Wycliffe Hall, Oxford, he came to this continent to join the faculty of Wycliffe College, Toronto. Both in Canada, and in the United States where he moved in 1919, Dr. Griffith Thomas became widely known as an outstanding Bible teacher, preacher and lecturer.

His *Devotional Commentaries* on *Genesis* and *Romans*, and his volume entitled *The Apostle Peter* were published originally by the Religious Tract Society of London. They had been out of print for some time, as had also *The Apostle John*, first published by The Sunday School Times Company, and *Grace and Power*, first published by Fleming H. Revell Company, when because of their continuing value and the demand for them on the part of the Christian public, new American editions were arranged.

After the author's death in 1924, Mrs. Griffith Thomas, who survived him until 1953, and their daughter continued to make America their home. The latter, now Mrs. E. H. Gillespie, having edited *Sermon Outlines* (1947), *Outline Studies in the Gospel of Luke* (1950), *Outline Studies in the Acts of the Apostles* (1956), *Through the Pentateuch Chapter by Chapter* (1957), i- tinuing the preparation of her father' lical notes for early publication.

Sermon Outlines

Sermon Outlines

Exegetical and Expository

BY

W. H. Griffith Thomas, D.D.

WM. B. EERDMANS PUBLISHING CO.

Grand Rapids   1956   Michigan

SERMON OUTLINES: EXEGETICAL AND EXPOSITORY
by W. H. Griffith Thomas, D.D.

Set up and printed, January, **1947**
Fourth printing, September, 1956

CONTENTS

Sermon Outlines

1.

The Godly Life

2 KINGS 18:5-7—*"He trusted in the Lord God of Israel; so that after him was none like him among all the kings of Judah, nor any that were before him. For he clave to the Lord, and departed not from following him, but kept his commandments, which the Lord commanded Moses. And the Lord was with him; and he prospered whithersoever he went forth."*

THE godly life is much the same essentially, at all times. These verses summarize Hezekiah's life before they enter upon the details of it. They sum up our life also. What are the secrets of all true life?

I. *Trusting* — "He trusted in the Lord God of Israel" (v. 5)

   1. The Old Testament has much on trust, and in the New Testament there is pre-eminently Hebrews 11.

   2. Note various aspects:
      (a) English: trusting to — on — in.
      (b) Hebrew: credit — lean on, roll on, devolve, commit, stay, take refuge.

   3. Here the significance of the word is to lean on God as a foundation — as a cripple leans hard on crutches, for use.

11

4. Compare Hezekiah and Sennacherib as illustration.

   (a) Hezekiah taunted with his trust.

   (b) Yet he spread the letter before the Lord.

5. God the foundation bedrock of all life.

II. *Cleaving* — "He clave to the Lord" (v. 6)
   1. The figure — adhesion.

   2. The usages — bone and skin, girdle and loins, tongue and mouth, man and wife, Israel and God, Ruth and Naomi.

   3. The meaning.
      (a) Adherence of loyalty.
      (b) Adhesion of love.
      (c) Adhesiveness of fellowship.

   4. The application.
      (a) Twofold aspect — resistance, persistence, vigorous tenacity.
      (b) Separation from and attachment to — nothing to separate from God — each day closer.

III. *Following* — "Departed not from following Him" (v. 6)
   1. Note paradox of contact and pursuit.

   2. Compare Psalm 63: "My soul thirsteth" (v. 1); "my soul shall be satisfied" (v. 6); "my soul followeth hard" (v. 8).

   3. Always near and yet ever closer.

IV. *Obeying* — "Kept His commandments" (v. 6)
   1. The outcome of all is practical obedience.

   2. Guard against two errors:
      (a) Stopping short of obedience.
      (b) Thinking of obedience only.

V. *Realizing* — "And the Lord was with him" (v. 7)
   Emphasize the "and" — cause and effect.
   1. The Presence of God.

   2. The Prosperity of the Godly.

Conclusion
   1. Faith

   2. Fellowship

   3. Following

   4. Faithfulness

   5. Feeling

2.

The Christian Life (I)

PSALM 16:8—*"I have set the Lord always before me: because He is at my right hand, I shall not be moved."*

THE Christian life is very simple if properly understood. It may be reduced to one single truth. It must be nothing less and can be nothing more than the realization of the presence of God in daily life. Psalm 16:8 is an illustration of this. It is golden with the realization of God as a Present Reality leading to Future Glory. God is real now and ever.

I. *The Required Effort.* Personal Surrender.
   1. What? "The Lord . . . before me."
   2. When? "Always."
   3. How? "Set" — effort needed to keep in touch. To form a habit needs diligence. Then it will come easily.

II. *The Resulting Effect.* Perpetual Strength.
   1. Protection — against all.
   2. Power — for all.
   3. Peace — in all.

Time of business not less blessed than time of prayer. I may possess God in noise of kitchen or workshop in as great tranquillity as in quiet of Communion.

14

III. *The Realized Experience.* Perfect Satisfaction.

    1. In relation to our own selves, which are change-able. God is greater than ourselves.

    2. In relation to our circumstances, which are vari-able. God is above the fog and clouds of life.

    3. In relation to our sins, which are terrible. God has condemned them (Rom. 8:3).

Conclusion

    1 How is this to be obtained?
      (a) By faith introducing us into God's presence.
      (b) His salvation first.

    2. How maintained?
      (a) Faith — Fellowship — Faithfulness.
      (b) Begin each day with God.

The Christian Life (II)

PSALM 16:7, 8, 11—"*I will bless the Lord, who hath given me counsel. . . . I have set the Lord always before me. . . . Thou wilt show me the path of life.*"

THE Christian life is summed up in the Realized Presence of God (v. 8). The Life Hereafter will be the Reality of the Presence of God (v. 11). The whole of Psalm 16 develops from the present into the future. It is clearer about the future than almost any other part of the Old Testament. Why is the future secure? Because of the experience of God's presence here. It is sure to continue. Personal experience is the sure basis of immortality.

See connection between verses in following parallels:

The Lord my Teacher (v. 7)	The Lord my Leader (v. 11)
The Lord before me (v. 8)	I before the Lord (v. 11)
The Lord at my right hand (v. 8)	I at the Lord's right hand (v. 11)

1. *God Our Counsellor*

   Here (v. 7), hereafter (v. 11). A traveler needs a guide along the way. The Lord will be our Guide not only at the end of life but all along. It is "life" even if it dip into the valley of the shadow (vs. 9, 10). How personal it is! — "Thou . . . me." Sufficient Light here — Perfect Light hereafter. All problems are mitigated here and will be solved there in the presence of God.

II. *God Our Companion*

Our faces toward God here — His face toward us there. "Face" denotes presence, nearness, grace. "There" is continuation and crown of "here." New methods of manifestation but same God. New capacities of apprehension for us.

III. *God Our Crown*

He at our right hand now — steadfastness
We at His right hand then — satisfaction
"Right hand" represents favor, honor, glory. Compare Matthew 25 — sheep and goats.
Emphasis on nouns in verse 11 — "path of life" — "fulness of joy" — "pleasures for evermore."

Conclusion

How begin? — Verse 1 — I trust
How go on? — Verse 6 — I have
     Verse 7 — I will
     Verse 8 — I set
     Verse 9 — I rejoice

How end? — Verse 10 — Thou wilt not
     Verse 11 — Thou wilt

4.

The Face of God

PSALM 27:8—*"When thou saidst, Seek ye my face; my heart said unto thee, Thy face, Lord, will I seek."*

WE can only think of God in terms applicable to man. These are the highest we have or can have at present; so we read of different parts of the human body applied to God. Compare Bible anthropomorphism. Feet indicate progress (Gen. 3:8; 2 Cor. 6:16); hand, work (Neh. 2:8; Eccles. 2:24); arm, strength (Deut. 33:27; Mark 10:16); mouth, speech (Deut. 8:3; Matt. 4:4). Chief of all, the face of God is mentioned (Exod. 33:11; Deut. 34:10). As the face is a most important part of man, so references to God's face are most suggestive.

I. *God's Presence*

    1. The word "face" is used for God's Person and Presence

        (a) Cain fled from the face of God. "Hide face" — lose sense of presence — Jacob, Manoah.

        (b) Old Testament word "presence" — face (Exod. 33:14; Psa. 16:11).

        (c) Shewbread — of face — Angel of His face (Isa. 63:9).

        (d) So face — presence. Photograph of someone is good, but presence better.

2. God's Presence all in all to us.
   (a) Salvation (Psa. 42:5); Rest (Exod. 33:14);
   Power (Psa. 114:7); Protection (Psa. 31:20);
   Joy (Psa. 21:6).
   (b) Courage (Isa. 43:2); Success (Josh. 1:5);
   Heaven (Rev. 22:3, 4).
   (c) So contrary: Cain (Gen. 4:14); Samson
   (Judg. 16:20); David (Psa. 51:11); Destruc-
   tion (2 Thess. 1:9); Sin (Isa: 59:2).

II. *God's Will*
   1. The word "face" expresses God's Will, Desire,
   Purpose.
      (a) A look or word — almost every indication
      by face.
      (b) Approval, displeasure, wish, indifference.

   2. God's Will needed by us
      (a) His Word — "speak" — "I will hear" — "in-
      quire"
      (b) His Fellowship (Psa. 32:8); Light (Psa.
      44:3).
      (c) So contrary — "set face against" — "rebuke
      of countenance" (Psa. 80:16). Cf. Psa.
      89:15; 90:8.
      (d) Good shown by light of countenance (Psa.
      4:6).

III. *God's Character*
   1. The word "face" is used to denote an index of
   character
      (a) Physiognomy if not phrenology shows
      whether weak, fickle, strong, good.
      (b) We find much in a perfect human face —
      so also and more in God's face.

2. God's character to be received and reproduced.

   (a) Light: intellectual and moral (Rev. 1:16).
       A face "lit up" is full of intelligence and
       sincerity.

   (b) Warmth, sympathy, interest, love.

   (c) Cf. (a) and (b): if only (a) possessed —
       over-anxiety; if only (b) possessed — too
       great vivacity; but combination brings rest
       and peace and often real beauty.

   (d) Strength — balances other three — or else
       faulty.

   (e) All four make up good face — so also God:
       Truth — Love — Peace — Power.

   (f) This is for us if we seek (Psa. 24:6) — "be-
       holding" (2 Cor. 3:18; Num. 24:17).

Conclusion

   What? Dwell in His Presence
         Discover His Will
         Delight in His Character
   How? Seek (1 Chron. 16:11)
         Abide (Psa. 11:7, R.V.)
         Pray (Psa. 31:16)
         Look (Jude 21)
         Obey (Psa. 89:15)

   In the Present (Acts 6:15)
   In the Future (1 Cor. 13:12)

5.

God Our Home

PSALM 91:1—*"He that dwelleth in the secret place of the most High shall abide under the shadow of the Almighty."*

FEW words have such a sweet, strange power as "Home." "No place like home." It is not quite accidental that the French language has no word for "home." Three sweetest, purest, dearest words in the English language are said to be: "Jesus — Mother — Home." Here we have "God our Home" (vs. 1, 9). Compare Psalm 90:1 and take opening verses of two Psalms together: death (Psa. 90) and life (Psa. 91), and God our Home the secret of both. Our text is a Hebrew parallelism, not an example of tautology: it represents our duty and God's acknowledgment — loving faith answered by faithful love.

I. *The Believer's Life*
   1. His Divine Relationship — "Most High" — Cf. use in Genesis 14 and occasionally throughout Old Testament. Denotes God's Separateness, Supremacy, Majesty and Holiness.

   2. His Privileged Position — "secret place" — word used in various ways: e.g., David's hiding-place — central tent of general (Psa. 31:20) — Holy of Holies in Tabernacle (Psa. 27:5) — i.e., union and communion with God. All this in Christ

21

(Isa. 9:6 — Wonderful, or secret). Cf Greek mystery.

(a) Secret of Word of God. Cf. cursory reading of letter or book and entering into thought and heart of writer.

(b) Communion with God. Cf. talking and having fellowship. Some souls never able to enter the "secret place."

(c) Love of God. Cf. respect and love — esteem and affection.

(d) Purpose of God. Cf. making plans with acquaintance and fellowship with co-workers.

3. His Constant Attitude — "dwelleth" — fixed, settled, habitual abode — "in Christ" (Eph. 1:10), "in Me" (John 15:2, 4, 5, 6, 7). Cf. habit and habitation, so Christian life: as we abide we learn and enjoy secrets of the Lord. Press this: two classes of Christians — (1) at home in the world and "visit" Christ; (2) at home in Christ and "visit" the world. "In" the world but not "of" it.

II. *The Believer's Powers*

1. His Divine Strength — "Almighty" — not only mighty, but "mighty for all," for everything.

2. His Perfect Provision — "shadow" — protection, shadow of hand; refreshment, shadow of rock. Both indicate peace and serenity of soul.

3. His Continual Abode — "abide"

(a) The Word of God his protection — when assailed, his sword.

(b) Fellowship with God — raises impulses, tastes, desires to higher sphere. Cf. cultured and ignorant men.

(c) Love of God — his soul impregnated and preserved.

(d) Purpose of God — his own purpose enlarged and ennobled — different view of life.

Conclusion

Life, therefore, need be neither arbitrary nor uncertain, but according to fixed, positive law. It has the absolute security of the man who makes God his dwelling place.

1. A Possibility for All (v. 1)

2. A Fact in One (v. 2)

(a) "My" — appropriation of faith.

(b) Then action of faithfulness.

(c) Fulfil conditions and God will follow with consequences.

(d) "He who will make God his shelter by day shall have God's protection at night" (Heb.).

> I would commune with Thee, my God,
> E'en to Thy seat I come;
> I leave my joys, I leave my sins,
> And seek in Thee my home.
>
> I stand upon the mount of God
> With sunlight in my soul,
> I hear the storms in vales beneath,
> I hear the thunders roll;

But I am calm with Thee, my God,
  Beneath these glorious skies,
And in the height on which I stand
  Nor storms nor clouds can rise.

Oh, this is life! Oh, this is joy,
  My God, to find Thee so,
Thy face to see, Thy voice to hear
  And all Thy love to know!

6

The Feeding of the Five Thousand (I)

MATTHEW 14:18—*"Bring them hither to me."*

THIS is the only miracle recorded in all four Gospels. Why? It was a turning-point in the ministry of Christ. It marked the end of the year in Galilee, the preparatory stage of His ministry, and introduced His real work. It was a crowning hour and yet to Jesus was a sad and bitter hour, for in spite of the miracle many went away, and only the few remained. In this miracle was a symbol of the work of Christ (see John 6).

I. *The Perishing World*

1. Weakness — Then, through lack of physical food; now, through sin and loss of presence of God.

2. Weariness — Then, it was evening and the crowds had journeyed far; now, the world is jaded from wandering.

3. Want — Then, of evening meal, for when hungry nothing but food satisfies; now, "Thou hast made us for Thyself, and our hearts are restless till they rest in Thee."

II. *The Powerless Church*

1. Insufficiency — Then, of food to supply crowds; now, of spiritual resources for a starving world. All that could be done in human power was to "send away." But where? It is the same today. But again, where? (See John 6:68).

2. Inability — Then, to buy food. Was it money or opportunity that was lacking? Perhaps both. Now, in the presence of heathenism, pagan civilization, indifference, worldliness, sin — no spiritual food to offer. Our shameful condition unwarranted by available provision of grace.
The Request — "Send them away"; the Reminder — "Give ye"; the Rejoinder — "What are they" (See John 6:9).

III. *The Perfect Saviour*

1. The Command — "bring." There must be sacrifice, complete and lasting — absolute obedience.

2. The Secret — "to Me." The disciples were in the presence of Power Incarnate.

3. The Blessing — "blessed." Work ineffectual without benediction of the Father.

4. The Supply — "they did all eat and were filled." Even fragments left over; was it coincidence that there were twelve baskets, as well as twelve disciples?

Conclusion

Christ could have performed this miracle without assistance from His disciples. But He chose to work through them, and He chooses today to work through us. Instruments must be fully yielded. Christian work is in exact proportion to the devotion of God's people. Christ must be all in all or not at all.

7.

Opportunity or Failure?

MATTHEW 14:18—*"Bring them hither to Me."*
MATTHEW 17:17—*"Bring him hither to Me."*

CHRISTIANITY may be defined as the full contact of the soul and Christ. Look at it now as illustrated by two episodes: (1) The disciples face to face with a great work; (2) the disciples face to face with a great failure. When we are confronted with either opportunity or failure, Christ says: "Bring . . . to Me."

I *Our Opportunities*

1. The Great Need — The People
   (a) Hunger and fatigue — want and weakness
   (b) No supply at hand

2. The Small Store — The Disciples
   (a) Limited
   (b) Insufficient

3. The Full Supply — The Master
   (a) Brought
   (b) Blessed

N.B. — The secret of today in the means of today for the task of today is that service is not measured by our ability but by His power.

28

II. *Our Failures*

    1. The World — The Father and the Multitude
        (a) Disappointed
        (b) Distressed

    2. The Church — The Disciples
        (a) Utter failure — no need for it
        (b) Unwarranted faithlessness — no right to it

The Master
    (a) Overruling
    (b) Explaining

N.B. — The task of today is great; the means of today are ample; the secret of today is faithfulness.

Conclusion

    1. Christianity does not give inherent ability.

    2. But it does ask for maintained dependence — the secret of salvation first, and then of holiness and power. This is the great safeguard against all danger.

> I take, He undertakes
> I have faith, He is faithful
> I trust, He is trustworthy

8.

The Feeding of the Five Thousand (II)

MARK 6:37—*"Give ye them to eat."*

THE importance of this episode in the life of Christ is indicated by its presence in all four Gospels, the only miracle so recorded. It is connected with the disciples' report of the death of John the Baptist and their return from their first preaching tour.

I. *A Busy Time* (vs. 30-34)

1. Both they and their Master needed rest. Both Lord and worker had wrought and taught many things.

2. They were under great pressure and were greatly needed.

3. Amid gathering crowds, Christ was calm. This was the time for sowing, not reaping.

4. He had a deep compassion for the crowds. This was ever Christ's way.

II. *A Pressing Need* (vs. 35-38)

1. The place was uninhabited, hence no source of food.

2. The time was late.

3. The need was great — 200 pence equal to about $24.

4. The supply was scanty, if reckoned without Christ. But duty is not measured by human ability but by divine enabling.

III. *A Full Supply* (vs. 39-44)

1. Orderly arrangement; it took faith on the part of the disciples to seat the crowds and on the part of the crowds to sit down when bidden.

2. Devout testimony to the Father by the blessing of the food.

3. General bestowal upon the multitudes.

4. Entire satisfaction, not partial. Significance of twelve basketfuls remaining may have been for each of the disciples to have his rightful share.

Conclusion

1. Christ's Motive — compassion. On the suffering multitudes and also on the disciples' faith. Christ is concerned with both spiritual and physical needs.

2. Christ's Manner — calmness. There was no fear, but rather an attitude of full sufficiency.

3. Christ's Method — cooperation. It was through the disciples that He worked on this occasion; it is through believers that He works today.

His Compassion, Capability, Care — beyond our need, our merit, our comprehension.

9.

The Parable of the Rich Fool

Luke 12:16, 20—*"The ground of a certain rich man brought forth plentifully. . . . But God said unto him, Thou fool."*

THERE were sharp contrasts among Christ's hearers, expressive of every attitude from passive indifference, through dawning interest, to either deep devotion or downright hostility. Here is the record (Luke 11:14 to 13:9) of a continuous discourse, during which there are several interruptions or interpolations. One of them (12:13) was the occasion for a parable illustrative of Christ's teaching against the sin of covetousness.

I. *The Spirit of Covetousness* (vs. 13-15)

A. *Manifested* (v. 13).

   1. The circumstances are a matter for conjecture. The inquirer's cause may have been just or it may not. The elder brother's portion was supposed to be double that of the younger. Probably the claim in this case was right but the spirit behind it was wrong, for the following reasons:

      (a) Unusually blunt exhibition of worldliness, especially considering Christ's words immediately preceding. The hearer seized upon his reference to the law and pricked up his ears.

(b) It was his need which prompted his speech, and he thought he saw a chance to get the benefit of the law gratis and win his case.

(c) To him, therefore, Christ was only a good lawyer. There was no response from the spiritual side of his nature. He was listening to God Incarnate and yet there was no stirring in his soul.

(d) Often so with us: we are off on the stream of our own plans while we seem to be listening to Christ's message, and so His words fall off our consciousness, leaving no effect behind.

(e) This man judged a situation by his own wishes and cravings; how often we do likewise!

(f) Many are ready to call Christ Master for their own advantage: Illustrations: beggar at minister's door, promising glibly to come to church; boy at Sunday School with idea of getting good position through influence; those who attend services for what they can get — "rice Christians," as such are known in Orient.

(g) But saying "Master" or "Lord" does not make a disciple.

2. Christ refuses the request, disapproving, as it were, the mixing of religion and politics, things spiritual and things temporal, in the man's mind. He is thinking of two ways of change — external and internal. The first is apt to leave

conditions, cases and even men as they were before; the second changes man himself and thus conditions and cases are also changed. An instance is the question of holiness. Love in the heart makes for new conditions because of a new character. In the spiritual sphere, love and truth adjust the personality to its highest form.

B. *Shunned* (v. 15)

1. Covetousness appears in many forms. Compare two:
   (a) Clutching what is already possessed.
   (b) Grasping for more.

2. "Take heed" — "beware"
   (a) It has a stealthy approach.
   (b) It has a terrible end.

C. *Condemned* (v. 15)

1. *An Incontestable Fact*

   Worldly goods cannot keep the soul alive. Not even an abundance of them can do this, since in this case abundance is no better than mere sufficiency.

2. *A Humbling Fact*
   (a) If life is primarily spiritual, not what it has but what it is counts.
   (b) "How much is he worth?" is a question often asked. It should apply more to character than to possessions.
   (c) Man distinct from his possessions and cannot amalgamate with them. Possible to buy books and yet be illiterate. All depends on capacity.

3. *An Inspiring Fact*

There is hope for those who recognize these distinctions.

II. *The Course of Covetousness* (vs. 16-19)

A. *A Worldling* (v. 16)

The rich man of Christ's parable was doubtless considered a provident, enterprising and influential citizen — the sort of person who nowadays would preside at meetings and to whom hats would be doffed with great respect. He was an example of "getting on in life," one "looked up to." But his story gives us an insight into the great problem of the rich — wondering where to invest his money. He had not seen the "prospectus" of Proverbs 19:17: "He that hath pity upon the poor lendeth unto the Lord; and that which he hath given will He pay him again."

B. *His Worldly Goods* (v. 16)

1. They were not gained wrongly; sin came after gain.

2. It is not sin to have, only to hoard.

C. *His Worldly-Wise Attitude* (vs. 17-19)

His Meditation (v. 17)

(a) There was difficulty in the project.

(b) He consulted no one. What he had was not a godsend, but a windfall.

2. His Mistakes (vs. 18, 19)

(a) He mistook Body for Soul

(1) Production — cultivated his land well — no objection to that. Ship should be in water, but not water in ship.

(2) Prosperity — model farmer, showing industry and diligence — success a great test — still no objection.

(3) Pondering — what to do with accumulated wealth — still not essentially wrong unless accompanied by undue anxiety or selfishness.

(4) Proposal — eating important to him — here he errs, in thinking exclusively of body — souls do not eat, nor live by bread alone. In such a life there is often chaff for the starving mind: money, athletics, pleasure, position, business success, but no spiritual satisfaction.

(b) He mistook Self for God

(1) Consideration — with himself — no other counsel. There should be thought but not of self alone.

(2) Center — "I" — "all my" — the first person is often the Devil's own pronoun which, if used exclusively, shuts out God and brother-man alike.

(c) He mistook Time for Eternity

(1) Anticipation — "years" — he could lay up goods but not time.

(2) Announcement — no mention of "if the Lord will."

III. *The Penalty of Covetousness* (vs. 20, 21)

A. *Classed with Fools* (v. 20)

A fool is utterly devoid of mind — so this man's sagacity much in question.

B. *Cut off from Life* (v. 21)

He thought of years but could not reckon on one night. "It is certain we can carry nothing out" (1 Tim. 6:7).

C. *Poor for Eternity* (v. 21)

He left all behind — except himself and he was worthless.

Conclusion

A. *The Sin*

1. Covetousness is not confined to the wealthy.

   (a) Wealth measured by position and claims.

   (b) Any man wealthy who finds he has more than enough.

   (c) Love of gain in poor man is as serious as sin of rich man here.

2. Covetousness is self first in everything

   (a) Pleasure — Comfort — Indulgence — Protection, — in a word, Selfishness.

   (b) This is possible in all, rich or poor, small or great.

B. *The Remedy*

1. Denial of Self

   (a) The word "deny" has two meanings — refuse and ignore.

   (b) Compare Peter's denial of Christ —he disowned and he repudiated. Our attitude to self should be as strong as this, and it should be shown daily.

2. Displacement by Christ

This will be accomplished by

(a) Crowning Him as Lord;

(b) Being concerned with Him — absorbed in Him — doing His will;

(c) Perpetual recognition of Him — nothing apart from Him;

(d) Having not one penny nor ten minutes — except in Him.

Thus was Christ Himself in His devotion to the Father. To assert self is to displace Christ. To displace by Christ is to deny self. So let us yield, abide, obey, that "in all things He might have the pre-eminence."

10.

The Parable of the Loving Father

LUKE 15:21, 22—*"Father, I have sinned. . . . But the Father said . . ."*

THIS should be called "The Parable of the Loving Father" rather than "The Parable of the Prodigal Son." It has also been referred to as "The Pearl of Parables."

In Scripture, the words "I have sinned" are said by eight different men. Four times they are said without reality:— by Pharaoh, Balaam, Saul, Judas. Four times they are said in sincerity:— by Job, Achan, David, the Prodigal Son. Of these, the last instance is the most notable for us, since we are told the steps to and from the utterance of the phrase. We are given the history of a sin, with the experience of the sinner made very clear.

I. *Downward* — Seven Steps

1. *Restraint.* Life is bright with every opportunity, but the son of the home was under law, the rules of the household. Not license (abuse of law) but liberty (regulated freedom). So man and God — freedom within bounds (Gen. 3:2, 3).

2. *Restlessness.* Son not satisfied — chafed — hemmed in — wanted to get away from father and home — could not find enjoyment. So man, in

natural state, incapable of finding fullest enjoyment in God.

3. *Request.* Emphasis on the word "me." Wanted goods, not presence or love of father. Unlawful because not yet due, but was determined on freedom. So man wants to be let alone, to be "free."

4. *Responsibility.* Granted — now own master — free to do as he liked. So sinful nature — self-will — independence of God. "Portion" — endowments of life. Sin makes man want to be lord of himself and his possessions.

5. *Recklessness.* Off at once — waste — riotous living — no thought of responsibilities — freedom only consideration — has his "fling" — sin always wastes — living for self is waste.

6. *Retribution.* Famine — "harmony with environment" a principle of moral law. Tendency of sin or virtue to gather corresponding surroundings. Fortune goes, famine comes. Life within and circumstances without agree.

7. *Reproach.* Menial task for Jew to be swineherd, especially when employed by "citizen" of another country. No friend near — everyone left when all was gone. Isolation of sinner — homelessness. Degradation of sinner — emptiness.

   Germ of Sin — self-will — emptiness.
   Growth of Sin — gradual, not precipitate.
   Goal of Sin — separation from God.

II. *Upward* — Seven Steps
   1. *Reflection.* "Came to himself" — so before he was "beside himself" (madness of heart). "Said"

41

— or thought (talking to himself) and first thought was of his father and the servants of the household. First step up is always realization of others than self.

2. *Recollection.* Past comes before him — the conditions he abandoned so carelessly. Servants better off than himself now. Second step is letting memory work.

3. *Realization.* "I perish" — no blame to any but self. Third step is to stop blaming others.

4. *Resolution.* "I will arise" — "I will do" — "I will say." Conversion is "turning around" and starting off in the opposite direction.

5. *Repentance.* Means entire turning. Forsaking of sin necessary to prove reality.

6. *Restoration.* Cf. attitudes in meeting: the son "held himself afar" but the father "ran." No rebuke — "not 'forgiven' but 'loved'" as far as expression was concerned. Reconciliation included robe, ring, shoes — all showing sonship.

7. *Rejoicing.* Love requited brings joy. So joy in heaven and in the heart of God over "one sinner that repenteth."

Grace of God — Longing and watching love — quick reconciliation — full welcome — entire restoration.

Greatness of God — Reconciliation possible because of God's character and Christ's atonement.

Glory to God — New life to prodigal, but better still if he had never wandered. Life of elder brother more exemplary — "ever with me" and "all that

I have is thine" — so in this story there is no premium on sin. But elder brother should have emulated father in attitude to returning prodigal.

Where are we? Going down, or going up? If down, why farther? God says, Return! Shall we not say, "Behold we come"?

Conclusion — The four characteristics of the prodigal's return as found in this chapter (Luke 15) were:

1. Conviction — "came to himself" (v. 17).
2. Confession — "I have sinned" (v. 18).
3. Contrition — "no more worthy" (v. 19).
4. Conversion — "he arose and came" (v. 20).

11.

The Christian Life

2 CORINTHIANS 9:8—*"God is able to make all grace abound toward you; that ye, always having all sufficiency in all things, may abound to every good work."*

ST. PAUL was always desirous that Christians should realize fully their possessions and possibilities. The Gospel speaks of inheritance and refers to present as well as future realization of it. The Greek word *"ploutos"* shows fulness of God for us.

Paul also keeps prominent the idea of a vigorous Christian life. He does this on every possible occasion and in connection with the simple facts of every-day living. Wherever opportunity offers, he drives it home by way of counsel, or encouragement, or warning, or command. Here, he urges his readers to liberality in sowing, or giving — "God loveth a cheerful giver" — and, consequently, in reaping, or getting — "God is able to make all grace abound." Thus the illustration leads up to the universal principle of the text, which has within it three great facts for every Christian.

I. *The Object of the Christian Life* — "that ye . . . may abound in every good work."

1. *Practical Living*

   a. Experience of Christianity in life—"by their fruits ye shall know them."

   b. Necessity — springing from "a true and lively faith."

   c. Good works — comparative, and so spiritual form for encouragement in each case.

2. *Consistent Living*

   a. "Every" — not some, but all.

   b. Two words: constant (time), consistent (truth).

   c. Our works neither constant nor consistent — are apt to be twisted — intervals between blessings — dangerous times.

   d. Physical life maintained by processes which never cease: lungs breathing, heart beating, etc. — but these are automatic and not dependent on the will, whereas the moral life needs will power.

   e. Is it possible to "will" good works? Scripture says yes, for the Christian; there is no excuse for inconsistency, and there is always the conscience, ready to admit a fault.

   Therefore, "every" good work: labor sometimes, play sometimes, sleep sometimes, eat sometimes — but "work" at all times. "Always" is one of Paul's favorite words.

2. *Unmistakable Life*

   Not meager, bare, poor — but should impress as something special. Should have abundance. Christianity was a new force in the world then and ought still to be seen as such.

II. *The Need of the Christian Life*

   1. *Present Resources* — "having . . . sufficiency"
      Cf. bankrupt — without means
      self-contained — above means

   2. *Sufficient Resources* — "all sufficiency"
      Never lacking — in home life, business life, church life.

   3. *Permanent Resources* — "always having all sufficiency"
      Always every energy — never taken unawares

III. *The Secret of the Christian Life*

   1. Supply of grace — not our own but God's own life in the soul.

   2. Variety of grace — "all" — Cf. Prayer Book Collect for 17th Sunday after Trinity — "given to all good works."

   3. Measure of grace — two "abounds" — God's grace abounds to us; then we abound to every good work.

   4. Adaptation of grace — "toward you" — "to every good work" — just what is required.

   5. Source of grace — God is able — grace depends on His character.

      a. Rely on God — assurance of faith

b. Abide in God — no waiting for new supply till old is exhausted — cf. automobile needing refilling with continuous supply of power to electric train or trolley-car.

c. Receive from God — "in-letting" before "out-letting."

12.

Thanksgiving

2 CORINTHIANS 9:15—*"Thanks be unto God for his unspeakable gift."*

THE Christian life has been called "a life of continual thanksgiving" — not simply thanksgiving at certain times but "continual" — "giving thanks always" (Eph. 5:20). In order for this we must realize what we have. St. Paul emphasizes thanksgiving throughout his writings and uses the phrase in our text, "Thanks be to God" four times (1 Cor. 15:57; 2 Cor. 2:14; 8:16; 9:15). All are veritable outbursts of gratitude. Even in Ephesians, where he was dealing with contradiction and opposition at their height, Paul had time and inclination to praise. Let us, therefore, look at *what* and *why,* so that we, too, may live this life of "continual thanksgiving."

I. *The Divine Gift*

1. *What?* Cf. John 4:10, "the gift of God"; Hebrews 6:4, "the heavenly gift"; with "his unspeakable gift" here.

   a. Christ — Eph. 4:7; Rom. 5:15, 17.

   b. The Holy Spirit — Acts 2:38.
   Both are to be received and possessed.

2. *What kind?* "His" — "unspeakable"
   a. Divine — nothing less — John 3:16; 2 Cor. 8:9.
   b. Inexpressible — indescribable because related to no other experience or possession.

II. *Gifts in the Divine Gift*
   1. *Loyalty*
      a. Surrender — 2 Corinthians 2:14, R.V. — "leadeth us in triumph" — thought is of captives led in triumphal procession.
      b. Service — Romans 6:17 — "ye have obeyed."

   2. *Love*
      a. Thought — 2 Corinthians 8:16 — consideration of others.
      b. Action — 2 Corinthians 8:17 — sympathetic cooperation with others.
      Cf. whole chapter, especially verse 9 — God's doing.

   3. *Life*
      a. Present Power — from dominion of sin (Rom. 7:25).
      b. Future Victory — from death (1 Cor. 15:57).

   4. *Labor*
      1 Timothy 1:12
      a. Equipped
      b. Recognized
      c. Authorized

Conclusion
   1. *The Spirit of a Thankful Life*
      a. Thankfulness in heart
      b. Thanksgiving in words
      c. Thanks-living in actions

49

2. *The Strength of a Thankful Life*
   a. Maintains fellowship — by the sweetening of prayer and the quickening of love.
   b. Preserves consistency — against murmuring and against pride.
   c. Energizes sympathy — freely received, so freely given.

3. *The Splendor of a Thankful Life*
   a. God's command obeyed (1 Thess. 5:18)
   b. God's gift recognized (Col. 1:12)
   c. God's glory maintained (2 Cor. 4:15)
   To "thank" we must "receive." Have we received Christ?

13.

Solicitude

LUKE 12:22-34—*"Take no thought . . . Consider . . . Seek not . . . Seek . . . Fear not."*

CHRIST often used general circumstances in specific cases. "Therefore" (v. 22), He says, trust is the antidote for a grasping spirit such as has just been under discussion (vs. 15-21). Let us take the word "solicitude" as the key to our study. A dictionary definition of a "solicitous" person is one who is "full of anxiety or concern, as for the attainment of something." There can be

I. *Vain Solicitude* (vs. 22-30).

We are told not to be vainly solicitous

A. *Because of the nature of life* (vs. 22, 23)
In 1611, Roger Bacon said, "A man died of thought." When anxiety prevails, sad looks and deep furrows tell. Anxiety wrong — same temper as "rich fool" in preceding verses — self-consuming care.

B. *Because of the care of the Creator* (vs. 24, 27, 28).
Ravens an interesting illustration — not eagles or nightingales, but birds of ill omen, birds of prey. Complete improvidence yet sure maintainence mark these inferior members of creation. Lilies — beauty as well as life — "much more" — food and raiment — all.

C. *Because of the uselessness of anxiety* (vs. 25, 26).
Does not go deep enough. Accomplishment greater without it. Foreboding opposite of foresight and destroys it.

D. *Because of pagan character of anxiety* (vs. 29, 30).
Brings discredit on God — as though He were not real and true. Little difference between this attitude and atheism — "a-theism" — "no-God-ism."

II. *True Solicitude* (vs. 31-34). We are told to "seek" the "kingdom of God."

A. *Because this attitude secures the present* (v. 31).
To "consider" and to "seek" brings "all these things."

B. *Because it assures the future* (v. 32).
Feebleness recognized — fearfulness forbidden — victory assured.

C. *Because it regulates life* (v. 33).
Scatter, yet increase. "God first" strikes balance.

D. *Because it insures character* (v. 34).
The heart follows its treasure. Picture in Paris of physicians examining dead body reminds us that death is always due to "absence of heart."

Conclusion

Key phrase, verse 29: "Neither be of doubtful mind." The Greek has the sense of not being tossed about on the open sea when one may be anchored safely in a roomy, sheltered haven.

1. *The Sea* — Care
Constant restlessness — dangerous instability — long separation

2. *The Anchor* — Trust
   Peaceful — safe — homelike
3. *The Harbor* — Fatherhood
   A relationship
   a. Endearing — "Father" — a delicate child is shielded
   b. Interested — "knoweth" — a timid child is encouraged.
   c. Individual — "ye" — an infirm child is helped.
   d. Enduring — "have need" — a tempted child is protected.

Therefore, trust all to "Our Father who art in Heaven," and rest in Him.

14.

Christian Character

COLOSSIANS 4:12—*"Stand perfect and complete in all the will of God."*

IT IS suggestive and may be significant that there is a seeming lack of emphasis in Paul's Epistles on an appeal to win or evangelize others — contra, 2 Timothy 4:5. But in writing to churches there is a constant emphasis on Christian life, character, and holiness, with the necessity of realizing full privileges. May there not be a connection between absence of one emphasis and reiteration of the other? If the inner life is right, soul-winning will be the natural and necessary outcome. As water finds its level, so our service, in quality, vitality and blessing, is never higher than the reality of our fellowship with God.

With this in mind, let us consider a prayer of one of Paul's companions, Epaphras, for his converts and friends, as recorded by the Apostle.

I. *The Elements of Christian Character*
   1. *Steadfastness* — "stand"
       a. Resistance against temptation and error.
       b. Persistence — painstaking work — e.g., Sunday School, Young People, visiting, witnessing.

   2. *Ripeness* — "perfect"
   Maturity realizes the end of our faith.

    a. Contrast "babe" of 1 Corinthians 3:1, 2 — un-ripeness

    b. Contrast "babe" of Hebrews 5:12, 13 — over-ripeness

    c. There should be the "happy medium" — with a clearness of spiritual perception, a charm of spiritual attractiveness, and a fruitfulness of spiritual influence.

3. *Assurance* — "complete"

    a. A.V. "fulfilled" — R.V. "fully assured,"

    b. Full assurance — faith, understanding, hope.

    c. Assurance of acceptance — possession.
                of fellowship — communion.
                of resources — provision.

II. *The Secret of Christian Character* — "in all the will of God"

  1. The will of God as the sphere of steadfastness, ripeness and assurance.

  2. The will of God as revealed in His Word
    a. By daily meditation.
    b. By hourly remembrance.
    c. By constant obedience.

Therefore: Learn, Love, and Live the Word, and find the secret of true Christian life and character.

15.

True Christianity

1 THESSALONIANS 5:1-28.

THIS Epistle should be read in connection with
Acts 17:1-14, which records Paul's visit to Thessalonica.
It was written at Corinth, shortly after Paul's departure,
and is probably the earliest of his letters. It mentions the
tidings he had received of the converts in Thessalonica
(1:6-10), and the reality of their Christian faith. Its di-
visions may be said to be two in number: Chapters 1-3,
Doctrine with Power; Chapters 4 and 5, Duty with Power.
This chapter, the fifth and last, is a summary of true
Christianity.

I. *What are the Marks of a Christian?*
   1. *Hopefulness* (vs. 1-10) — Looking onward
      a. Based on teaching (vs. 1-5).
      b. Marked by watchfulness (vs. 6-10).

   2. *Helpfulness* (vs. 11-15) — Looking outward
      a. Active endeavors (vs. 11-13).
      b. Varied endeavors (vs. 14, 15).

   3. *Happiness* (vs. 16-18) — Looking inward
      a. Joy (v. 16)
      b. Prayer (v. 17)
      c. Thanksgiving (v. 18)

4. *Holiness* (vs. 22, 23) — Looking upward
   a. Negative (v. 22)
   b. Positive (v. 23)

II. *How to Be a Christian*
   1. *By the Spirit of God* (v. 19)
      a. Not quenching His fire by sin.
      b. Not letting it go out by carelessness.

   2. *By the Word of God* (vs. 20, 21)
      a. Received (v. 20).
      b. Used (v. 21).

   3. *By Prayer to God* (vs. 17, 23, 25)
      a. Unceasing (v. 17).
      b. Definite (vs. 23, 25).

   4. *By Trust in God* (vs. 23, 24)
      a. His peace (v. 23).
      b. His preservation (v. 23).
      c. His faithfulness (v. 24).
      d. His fulfilment (v. 24).

16.

"Amen; Alleluia"

REVELATION 19:4—*"And the four and twenty elders and the four beasts fell down and worshipped God that sat on the throne, saying, Amen; Alleluia."*

TWO men met on board ship. One of them was from India and the other from China, and the language of each was unintelligible to the other. One man happened to say the word "Hallelujah!" and the other instantly responded, "Amen!" From that time on the voyage was an opportunity for fellowship, for they knew instantly that they had Christianity in common. What they may not have realized is that Christianity is summed up in these two words from the Hebrew which have been reproduced in almost every language on the globe.

"Amen" is a word indicating agreement or affirmation, and is found in innumerable passages of Scripture. "Hallelujah," or "Praise ye the Lord," is a word always associated with victory (see Psalm 104:35, where it first occurs in the Old Testament). The two words in conjunction are suggested in such passages as 1 Chronicles 16:36 and Nehemiah 5:12.

I. *God's Will Accepted* — "Amen"

   1. Literally, It is so, or, It shall be so; not, May it be so. It is a question whether the word is ever a supplication.

2. It is an affirmation, then, and a testimony to God's faithfulness.

   a. God's presence realized in everything — nothing apart from Him.

   b. God's purpose believed in everything — nothing fortuitous.

   c. God's power trusted in everything — that which He promised He is able to perform.

II. *God's Way Adored* — "Hallelujah"

  1. Because of the acknowledgment of God's wisdom.

  2. Because of trust in His power.

  3. Because of joy in His love.

Conclusion

  1. These two words are inseparable.
If first, then second (see Psalm 106:48).

  2. The order of the two is unchangeable.
Not second before or without first — conformity to, then confidence in, the Divine will and way.

  3. Their acceptance is inexhaustible.
It means receiving all from God and returning all to God. Since Christ is "God's Amen," in accepting Him we shall say our best and deepest "Hallelujah!"

17.

Jacob's Ladder

GENESIS 28:12—"*And he dreamed, and behold a ladder set up on the earth, and the top of it reached to heaven: and behold the angels of God ascending and descending on it.*"

THE ladder in Jacob's dream at Bethel stood for communication between God and man. There was and still is great need for this. Here is man on earth, and there is God in heaven. How shall they communicate with one another? Emerson's answer was, "Hitch your wagon to a star." But that is impractical, for here is my wagon and there, out of my reach, is the star. Even in this modern age of swift, easy communication, man has not bridged the chasm between earth and heaven. There is, therefore,

I. *The Need of Communication.*
   1. A ladder is a common article, but missed if unavailable. Used not only in the household but also in mountain-climbing, fire-fighting, etc.
   2. The distance between heaven and earth is as great in our day as in Jacob's. From Genesis 3 on, through Isaiah 6 and Luke 16, "there is a great gulf fixed." But what about

II. *The Means of Communication.*
   1. A ladder must be long enough. Jacob needed assurance of this.

2. Today men are making their own ladders: church membership, good works, orthodoxy. These are like Jacob's ladder in that they are all good and they all stand on the earth — but none of them can reach to heaven.

3. There is only one ladder which can — the Lord Jesus Christ — and He used this simile of Himself in John 1:51. Through Him there is both revelation and communion. But some may need proof, so note

III. *The Safety of Communication.*

1. A ladder must be strong enough. Can it bear weight?

2. The tests of Christ as Ladder beween earth and heaven may be thought of as steps, or rungs, five in number. At this end, He is Man (first rung); at the other end, He is God (fifth and last rung). In between: He must be a unique Man, and this uniqueness may be represented by His life, by His death, and by His resurrection and ascension (second, third and fourth rungs).

3. Since that time, millions have used this Ladder, and it has never even swayed under their weight. Then there is

IV. *The Freedom of Communication.*

1. The steps are convenient. The angels used Jacob's ladder and they are said to use "the Son of man" (John 1:51).

2. The steps are unobstructed. The angels
   a. Ascend with man's need and descend with God's provision.

    b. Ascend with man's prayer and descend with God's answers.

    c. Ascend with man's devotion and descend with God's acceptance.

Conclusion

1. Where else shall man find a means of communication with God? Christianity is the only faith which has one. Other religions have aspirants, but "a saviour not quite God is a bridge broken at the other end."

2. How shall we use this means of communication? The use of a ladder takes both hands and feet. J. G. Paton of the New Hebrides found the word in the native tongue nearest to our word "faith" was one which signified "leaning the whole weight." "Trust"— (feet) — and "obey"— (hands) .

3. Then let us up and use this Ladder! Let us, leaving earthly things behind, appropriate Christ as Saviour and Lord and Mediator. He offers us His presence, His protection, and His power — until we are welcomed into the Father's House.

"Higher still, and higher, bear the ransomed soul,
Earthly toils forgotten, Saviour, to its goal,
Where, in joys unthought of, saints and angels sing,
Never weary raising praises to their King!"

18.

Memories of Bethany

LUKE 10:38—"*He entered into a certain village.*"

JOHN 11:1—"*A certain man was sick, named Lazarus, of Bethany.*"

JOHN 12:1—"*Jesus six days before the passover came to Bethany.*"

LUKE 24:50—"*He led them out as far as to Bethany.*"

FOUR visits of Christ to Bethany are recorded. There He revealed Himself as

I. *The Gracious Teacher* (Luke 10:38-42)

1. *The Story*

   Delightful picture of home life — Christ resting. Cf. Mary and Martha. Both learned from the Master ("also," v. 39), but Martha was "cumbered" as well, so Jesus told her of the "one thing" needful. Even necessity may be a distraction, robbing of spirituality. Christ as Teacher was personal, patient, practical, and powerful.

2. *The Message.*

   Our knowledge of Him today often comes from various sources: books, papers, other Christians— "second-hand" — the difference between "knowing about" and "knowing." Therefore personal contact is necessary — not only for the sake of others, nor for our own intellectual benefit, but also for our spiritual growth and as defense against error. He also showed Himself to be

II. *The Sympathizing Friend* (John 11:1-45)

   1. *The Story*

   Delay in spite of words, "he whom Thou lovest" and "our friend Lazarus." There was a kind of anger in Christ's rejoinders because of implied reproach and failure in faith — even Mary (v. 32) — and Martha (v. 39) after her declaration in verse 22; and yet He sympathized (vs. 33-36).

   2. All agree on Christ's Humanity, but these disciples saw both His Humanity and His Deity in a few moments of time (vs. 33-36; 41-44). Cf. Hebrews 2:17; 4:15; 5:2 — Suffering, Temptation, Sympathy. We as Christians lose if we ignore His Humanity; although care should be taken. Cf. Fifth Commandment and Mariolatry. God dealing with our Sins and Man having Sympathy for us like the two trusses of a cantilever bridge.

   > "Thou knowest, not alone as God all-knowing,
   > As Man our mortal weakness Thou hast proved;
   > On earth with purest sympathies o'erflowing,
   > O Saviour, Thou hast wept and Thou hast loved;
   > And love and sorrow still to Thee may come
   > And find a hiding place, a rest, a home."

   Cf. "Able to save" (Hebrews 7:25)
   "Able to succor" (Hebrews 2:18)
   "Able to sympathize" (Hebrews 4:1)

   He was also shown to be

III. *The Suffering Saviour* (John 12:1-11)

   1. *The Story*

   The last full week of Christ's life on earth — His thoughts must have been full of what lay ahead —

His interpretation of Mary's anointing as they sat at farewell supper.

2. *The Message*
All through Scripture Christ is shown as "born to die" — so anointing typical of this.
In relation to God — righteousness, love, grace.
In relation to man — salvation, sanctification, satisfaction.

IV. *The Ascending Lord* (Luke 24:50-53)

1. *The Story*
Forty days between resurrection and ascension full of blessing for disciples. Ascension was crown of Christ's earthly experience (Heb. 1:3; Rom. 8:18). Churches which do not observe this holy day miss the culmination of His life on earth and the initiation of His life in heaven: "We do believe Thy only-begotten Son Lord Jesus Christ to have ascended into the heavens; so we may also in our heart and mind thither ascend, and with Him continually dwell" (Collect for Ascension Day).

2. *The Message*
Seven benefits from the Ascension:
a. Acceptance — unquestioned
b. Righteousness — untarnished
c. Life — unending
d. Peace — undisturbed
e. Relationship — unbroken
f. Title — undisputed
g. Inheritance — unfading

Conclusion

1. Christ the same now — Teacher, Friend, Saviour, Lord.

2. Is He ours? Principal Cairns called this a "personal transaction" — just as incidents in Bethany were on the more personal side of Christ's earthly life.

3. If so, we must

> Be much with Him
> Make much of Him
> Do much for Him

and Christ will be "all in all" because He is "Lord of all."

19.

A Bible Beacon — Lot

GENESIS 19:16—*"While he lingered . . . the Lord being merciful to him, they brought him forth."*

THERE are lives in Scripture which have been well called "beacons" because they are warnings: e. g., Balaam, Saul, Solomon. These men started out well, with every advantage and much promise, but ended in failure and even in disaster. Such a life was Lot's. His circumstances are well known: (a) with Abraham in Haran and Canaan (Gen. 11:31 to 12:9); (b) with Abraham in Egypt (12:10-20); (c) separated from Abraham (13:1-14); (d) rescued by Abraham (14:1-16); (e) last days in Sodom (19:1-16); (f) escape from Sodom and end of story (19:17-38). Lot's life is full of most solemn warning and valuable instruction for every Christian. Let us take time and opportunity for an examination of our own lives in comparison with his.

I. *Lot's Dangers*
   1. *Things Lawful*
      His emphasis on good land not wrong in itself — evil was in place in which he put it. "There are more killed by meat than by poison" — more lost through abuse of things lawful than through use of things unlawful. Possession is not wrong — being possessed by possessions is. Right for ship to be in water but not water in ship.

2. *Compromise*

Lot first moved "toward" Sodom (13:12), but soon "dwelt in" Sodom (14:12). We are not told of his actual going — perhaps gradual and almost imperceptible — but then we read that he "sat in the gate of Sodom" — i.e., was a great man there. Perhaps he thought to bear strong testimony — no use, for words not equal in effect to deeds (19:24), and he had evidently made money with the rest and shared their life. Should we go into the world to "influence" it? Never — it needs saving! Therefore there should be separation — in the world but not of it. First step in conformity with world bears a high price.

3. *Worldliness*

Lot did testify and was "vexed" (2 Pet. 2:7, 8) by wickedness, but also mixed hospitality and inter-marriage — essentially selfish. Some men cannot bear success — gives false position, influences home life, destroys opportunity for character-building. Lot not happy but, rather, very miserable.

II. *Lot's Needs*

1. *Independence*

All right while with Abraham, but not after. Prop removed, so he fell. Cf. ourselves minus our asso-ciations — church, business, friends. Best to culti-vate dependence not only on self but on God — spiritual life at firsthand.

2. *Decision*

Toward Sodom — rescued from Sodom — returned to Sodom — had to be hastened away — lingered — finally wrong decision, Zoar first instead of direct to mountains. For true life there is need for decisiveness and firmness. In test, result not as wished but according to preceding conduct. Character cannot be peeled off like skin or taken off like coat.

3. *Wholehearted Consecration*

Lot had come from Ur of the Chaldees with uncle, but had not made the same stand as to heathenism. Name means "veil." Was he (a) apparently godly but really worldly, or (b) worldly with tinge of religion, or (c) religious with taint of worldliness? Evidently last, for he is called "just" and "righteous" by Peter (2 Pet. 2:7, 8). So greatest need was for surrender, consecration, service.

Conclusion

1. *Lot's Life a Terrible Commentary*

   a. His end haunted by terror, both of sin of Sodom and of its punishment — sounded lowest depths of shame — sank into oblivion — death unrecorded — grave unknown — influence nil.

   b. But for words in New Testament, we should call him lost — but he is of those "saved yet so as by fire" (1 Cor. 3:15).

   c. Cf. Abraham — drawn to God's will by love and delight: Lot — driven by sorrow and discontent. Not in "by faith chapter" (Hebrews II), so no "good report by faith" (v. 39) and no abundant entrance (cf. II Pet. 1:5-11).

2. *Lot's Life a Trumpet Call*

   a. Keep close to God and His people — then sensitive to evil.

   b. Witness for God to world — then shining lighthouse, not half-way house.

"Resist! — Insist! — Persist!"

20.

Milestones

DEUTERONOMY 17:16—*"Ye shall henceforth return no more that way."*
JOSHUA 3:4—*"Ye have not passed this way heretofore."*

NEVER this way before — never this way again! Milestones are helpful, not only to show the way, but also as reminders of distance traveled and as encouragement for what is still to be covered. The New Year is a helpful milestone for past and future, although every day, according to Thomas Carlyle, is "the confluence of two eternities."

I. *Retrospect* (Deut. 17:16)
　1. *Sins*
　　Forgiven — covered — in spite of Satan's efforts. Cf. God's language — in the sea, behind His back, blotted out as a cloud, remembered no more.

　2. *Sorrows*
　　Discipline comes with discipleship — "nevertheless afterward" — estimate results, not processes, hills, not steps.

> "In the center of the circle
> Of the will of God I stand;
> There can be no second causes,
> All must come from His dear hand.
> All is well! for 'tis my Father
> Who my earthly life hath planned.

71

"Shall I pass through waves of sorrow?
Then I know it will be best;
Though I cannot tell the reason,
I can trust and so am blest.
God is love, and God is faithful,
So in perfect peace I rest."

3. *Mistakes*

It is well to

a. Cease regrets, for it is impossible to retrieve or retrace. Regret often weakens and opens way for "discouragement because of the way."

b. Profit by errors, and in this way decide on a different and better course.

II. *Prospect* (Josh. 3:4)

1. *New Opportunity*

New duties, new experiences, new ideas, new hopes, new determinations. It should be better, therefore, on before.

2. *New Assurance*

Cf. Numbers 9 and 10

Ark — presence of God
Pillar of cloud and fire — protection
Trumpets — precepts
Hobab — persuasion

3. *New Call*

Trust and obedience — faith and faithfulness — rest and love.

"With so blest a Friend provided
We upon our way would go,
Sure of being safely guided,
Guarded well from every foe.

> "Every day will be the brighter
>   When Thy gracious face we see;
> Every burden will be lighter
>   When we know it comes from Thee."

Conclusion

Therefore note these aspects of the will of God:

1. Purpose — "I came" (Heb. 10:7)
2. Aim — "I seek" (John 5:30)
3. Satisfaction — "my meat" (John 4:34)
4. Fellowship — "my brother" (Mark 3:35)
5. Prayer — "teach me" (Psa. 143:10)
6. Outcome — "for ever" (1 John 2:17)

Then note these aspects of the leading of God:

1. Start — "thou hast led forth" (Exod. 15:13)
2. Continuity — "he led him about" (Deut. 32:10)
3. Divinity — "the Lord also did lead" (Deut. 32:12)
4. Safety — "he led them on safely" (Psa. 78:53)
5. Obstacles — "he led them through the depths" (Psa. 106:9)
6. Direction — "he led them forth by the right way" (Psa. 107:7)

> "With the shade and with the sunshine,
>   With the joy and with the pain,
> Lord, I trust Thee—both are needed
>   Me, Thy wayward child, to train.
> Earthly loss, did we but know it,
>   Often means our heavenly gain."

21.

The Advent in the Thessalonian Epistles

I THESSALONIANS 5:23—*"The coming of our Lord Jesus Christ."*

THERE are three mountain peaks in the New Testament: the First Coming of Christ, the Coming of the Holy Spirit, and the Second Coming of Christ. Each is vitally important and should have due attention. The third of these is often neglected, even though it is mentioned 300 times in the New Testament. It is often thought that the Second Coming is impractical and has no bearing on life — and this in spite of 1 John 3:3 and 2 Peter 3:11, 14.

"There is nothing," says Dean Alford, "that so much takes a man out of himself; nothing that so much raises and widens his thoughts and sympathies; nothing that so much purifies and elevates his hopes, as this preparation for the coming of the Lord."

Of the earliest Epistles of Paul, seven are addressed to churches. These may be divided into four groups: those which have as their primary purpose (1) doctrinal foundation; (2) church life; (3) Christian experience; and (4) the coming of the Lord. In this fourth group are the two Epistles to the Thessalonians, of which every chapter treats of the Second Advent but one, and even that includes it indirectly. The Lord's Coming is shown to imply:

I. *Hope* (I, 1:3, 10)

1. Essential part of Christian life — all three, faith, hope and love, mentioned (v. 3).

2. Essential part of evidence proving original Gospel (v. 10).

II. *Work* (I, 2:17-19)

1. Present love of soulwinner (vs. 17, 18).

2. Future Prospect — association, presentation (v. 19).

III. *Holiness* (I, 3:12, 13)

Heart in Scripture includes mind, emotion and will, i.e., whole personality.

1. What? "Unblameable in holiness" — then.
   "Stablished in love" — now.

2. Where? "Before God."

3. When? "At the coming of our Lord Jesus Christ."

IV. *Comfort* (I, 4:13-18)

1. Problem (v. 13).

2. Solution (v. 14).

3. Revelation (vs.. 15-17).

4. Consolation (v. 18).

V. *Character* (I, 5:all)

1. *Edification* (vs. 1-11)
   "You" (vs. 1, 2); "they" (v. 3); "we" (v. 5); therefore, "let us" (vs. 6-8); "be sober" (vs. 6, 8) "in order to "edify" (v. 11).

    2. *Preservation* (vs. 12-14)

      a. Aspects of life (vs. 12-22).

      b. Anticipation of future (v. 23).

      c. Assurance of fulfilment (v. 24).

      d. Therefore, let us be alert, helpful, thorough.

VI. *Vindication* (II, 1)

    1. Rest after persecution (vs. 6, 7)

    2. Glory after opposition (v. 10).

VII. *Steadfastness* (II, 2)

    1. Information (vs. 1-12).

    2. Exhortation (vs. 13-17).

VIII. *Patience* (II, 3)

    Cf. verse 5 with James 5:8.

Conclusion

    Christ has come — Bethlehem
    Christ is coming — Pentecost
    Christ will come — Olivet

22.

"Here I Am"

ISAIAH 58:9—*"Thou shalt cry, and he shall say, Here I am."*
GENESIS 22:1—*"Abraham . . . said, Here I am."*
GENESIS 22:9—*"He said, Here am I, my son."*

THE smallest Bible in the world is said to measure in inches 1½ by 1 by ½. Yet the message of the Bible may be compassed in but three of the shortest words contained in it: "Here am I." What do we mean? Properly understood and used, these words include everything: in our first text, they were said by God to man; in our second text by man to God, and in our third, by man to man. Thus we may consider that they sum up that which comes *from* God, that which goes *to* God, and that which is done *for* God.

I. *From God* (Isa. 58:9)

Cf. context. The message prefigures the Gospel and emphasizes the presence of God in human life.

1. *Pardon*

His presence is salvation (Psa. 42:5, marg.)

a. *Historically.* Incarnation was God manifest in flesh. Illustration of Chinese catechist comparing Confucius, Buddha and Jesus Christ: Man in well — Confucius ignores him — Buddha is sorry for him but passes on — whereas Christ has a rope long enough to pull him out.

      b. *Individually.* Here and now, by means of Holy Spirit applying value of Christ's work — "nigh" (Rom. 10:8)

  2. *Power*

      a. *Guidance* — light — cf. pillar of fire — see John 8:12, "I am the light of the world: he . . . shall have the light of life."

      b. *Grace* — courage (Joshua) — success (Gideon). Our joy and confidence, moment by moment: "Here I *am*," not "will be."

  3. *Peace*

      a. *Companionship* — "In me . . . peace" (John 16:33) — "Lo, I am with you alway" (Matt. 28:20)

      b. *Hope* — "Christ in you, the hope of glory" (Col. 1:27).

How shall these things be? By the Word, and by the Spirit — these agree.

II. *To God* (Gen. 22:1)

  1. *Surrender*

      a. Letting go. Cf. Jacob (Gen. 31:11; 46:2).

      b. Laying hold. Cf. Jacob again (Gen. 31:26).

  2. *Service*

      a. Willingness. Cf. Isaiah (Isa. 6:8), Moses (Exod. 3:4).

      b. Preparedness — not "there" but "here."

  3. *Satisfaction*

      a. Possession — Cf. David (2 Sam. 15:26) — "I am His."

      b. Obedience — Cf. Our Lord (Matt. 26:39).

III. *For God* (Gen 22:7)
1. *Loyalty*
    a. Cf. Isaac to Abraham with Jacob to Isaac (Gen. 26:18).
    b. Service of others for Christ's sake (Eph. 6:7).

2. *Love*
    a. Cf. love of Abraham to Isaac with love of Isaac to Abraham — one yearning, the other trusting; one disposing, the other at disposal.
    b. Service because of love of others (Gal. 5:13).

3. *Labor*
    a. Work for the good of others (2 Cor. 12:15).
    b. Work for Christ (Col. 3:24).

Have we heard the One who says, "I am," responded "Thou art," and added, to others, "He is"?

Conclusion

"He said" — literally, definitely. Have we ever done so? The second "Here I am" is the pivot on which the first and third turn. God stands waiting; others have need; shall we not say to God, "Here I am!" — either for first time or afresh?

23.

Satisfaction

JEREMIAH 31:14—*"My people shall be satisfied with my goodness, saith the Lord."*

THE primary application of this promise from God is, of course, to Israel in the future. Yet a secondary and spiritual application may be made to the people of God in all ages.

I. *Our Choice Possession* — "My goodness"

This is another way of saying the *character* of God. Cf. Exodus 34:6; Rom. 11:22.

1. *It is seen in Nature.*
   a. Crowning the year with it (Psa. 65:11).
   b. The earth is full of it (Psa. 33:5).
   c. It endures continually (Psa. 52:1).

2. *It is seen in Revelation.*
   a. The Lord God is abundant in it (Exod. 34:6).
   b. It is made to pass before His servant (Exod. 33:19).
   c. Believers are satisfied with it (Psa. 65:4).
   d. It is part of the fruit of the Spirit (Gal. 5:22).

II. *Our High Possibility* — "shall be satisfied"

1. *Wrong views of satisfaction*
   a. To the worldling it means ease.

b. To the conventional man it provides an ordinary standard of living.

c. To the Pharisee it assures superiority.

d. To the Stoic it is a matter of indifference.

e. To the selfish man it brings no regard for others.

2. *The right view of satisfaction*

a. Bread for body never satisfies soul.

b. God alone can.

c. God alone does.

d. Ordinary desires intensified by sin need forgiveness and transformation — then come grace and glory.

e. "We have enough, yet not too much to long for more."

3. *The characteristics of satisfaction*

a. "With marrow and fatness" (Psa. 63:5).

b. "With mercy" (Psa. 90:14).

c. "With honey" (Psa. 81:16).

d. "With good things" (Psa. 103:5).

e. "With Thy likeness" (Psa. 17:15).

f. "With the bread of heaven" (Psa. 105:40).

g. "With long life" (Psa. 91:16).

4. *The recipients of satisfaction.*

a. "The meek" (Psa. 22:26).

b. "The poor" (Psa. 132:15).

c. "The longing soul" (Psa. 107:9).

d. "A good man" (Prov. 14:14).

5. *The time of satisfaction*

a. "In the days of famine" (Psa. 37:19).

b. "In drought" (Isa. 58:11).

      c. "When I awake" (Psa. 17:15).

      d. "Early" (Psa. 90:14).

"Wherefore do ye spend . . . your labor for that which satisfieth not?" (Isa. 55:2).

III. *Our Great Privilege* — "My people"

Once we were not His people — no relation. See, therefore,

1. *The conditions.*

      a. Mercy to be obtained (1 Pet. 2:10) — pardon

      b. Idolatry to be abandoned (2 Cor. 6:16) — purity

2. *The meaning.*

      a. "Peculiar people" (1 Pet. 2:9) means literally "people for a possession."

      b. A people, a name, a praise, a glory (Jer. 13:11).

Conclusion

Only God's "people" shall be "satisfied" with His "goodness." The possession of satisfaction means purity for the believer and praise for God. Is it yours? Do you belong to His people?

24.

Change

HOSEA 7:9—*"Gray hairs are here and there upon him, yet he knoweth it not."*

A FREQUENT order before battle is to "fire low," for it is a mistake to fire too high. Just as directness is needed in shooting, so the pulpit needs to use directness and plainness of speech, or its message will miss those for whom it is intended and fail to accomplish its purpose. Thus God's messengers in Bible times were direct in their speech — Nathan, the Prophets, John the Baptist, Paul — while in many ways Christ Himself was the greatest exponent of this principle in the entire Scriptures.

Our text exemplifies the tendency of man to be indefinite about his own deterioration and blind to change in himself.

I. *Change* — "gray hairs"

1. *A Fact*

   a. Life has different characteristics at each stage: infancy, youth, manhood, age.

   b. Gray hairs ordinarily sign of advancing years, of change, of incipient decay. "Change and decay in all around I see."

2. *A Reminder*
   a. Changes in life noticeable not only in appearance, but in temperament, feelings, circumstances.
   b. "This is not your rest" (Mic. 2:10). Earthly life not all.

II. *Gradual Change* — "here and there"
   1. *The Truth*
      a. Ordinarily not hurried, but gradual — so with other marks of age. Cf. eyesight — print often has to increase in size until the aged person returns to primer type he used in childhood.
      b. So with disease — often creeps up unnoticed.

   2. *The Teaching*
   Soul change may parallel body change.
      a. *The Sinner*
         (1) Dullness — hearing and seeing but not heeding.
         (2) Deafness to voice of God.
         (3) Dimness in seeing truth.
         (4) Deadness of life.
      b. *The Saint*
         (1) Less joy.
         (2) Less elasticity.
         (3) Less hopefulness.
         (4) Less taste for Bible-reading and prayer.
         (5) Less vitality in service.

III. *Unconscious Change* — "yet knoweth it not"
   1. *The Experience*
      a. Cf. literal knowledge, also symbolical.
      b. Workers past work and not know it.
      c. Incapacity to adapt to changing circumstances.

2. *The Truth*
   a. The sinner — ignorance of condition (Rev. 3:17); ignorance of opportunity (Luke 19:44).
   b. The saint — ignorance of opposite spiritual conditions. Cf. Moses (Exod. 34:29) and Samson (Judg. 16:20).

Conclusion

Physical change necessary — but spiritual change not.

Change for the worse may only be resisted by change for the better — spiritual renewal — either in salvation or in sanctification.

First unused and then unable. "How shall we escape if we neglect . . . ?" (Heb. 2:3).

Time must be "taken by the forelock" or it will "bear all its sons away." "Behold NOW!"

25.

The Christian Walk

Amos 3:3 — *"Can two walk together, except they be agreed?"*

THE Christian life is described and illustrated in Scripture by various actions of the body. Examples of this are as follows:

1. Seeing — "Look . . . and be ye saved" (Isa. 45:22).

2. Hearing — "Hear . . . and your soul shall live" (Isa. 55:3).

3. Grasping — "Take hold of My strength" (Isa. 27:5).

4. Tasting — "O taste and see that the Lord is good" (Psa. 34:8).

But perhaps the commonest, the most suggestive and the most complete figure of speech for the Christian life is that of Walking. It is of frequent occurrence in both Old and New Testaments, as for instance in the Epistle to the Ephesians, where it is used seven times (2:2; 2:10; 4:1; 4:17; 5:2; 5:8; 5:15).

Walking is one of two or three perfect forms of exercise, said to utilize all the muscles of the human body (cf. swimming and bed-making). It is therefore appropriate as applied to Christianity, which deals with the entire life of man. Our text has its primary application in the relation between God and His ancient people, and since that is one of the things written aforetime for our learning we may properly apply the figure, not only to the marriage relation, as is so often done, but also to the Christian life, the relation between Christ and the believer.

I. *The Nature of the Christian Life*

 1. *A Walk*

   Implies four things:

   a. Life — only those who live can walk.

   b. Activity — primary expression of life.

   c. Health — only the strong can "rise up and walk."

   d. Progress — not standing still.

   e. Destination — not a saunter with no object, nor yet a spurt with no staying power.

 2. *A Walk Together*

   Not a solitary existence. Cf. prepositions used in Scripture in connection with walking:

   a. "With" (Gen. 5:22) — companionship

   b. "Before" (Gen. 17:1) — sincerity

   c. "After" (Deut. 13:4) — obedience

   d. "In" (Col. 2:6) — union

 3. *Two Walking Together*

   a. Intimacy, fellowship (1 John 1:3).

   b. Reciprocal knowledge (1 Cor. 13:12); reciprocal love (John 15:12); reciprocal endeavor (2 Cor. 6:1).

   c. Steps in unison (2 Cor. 6:14).

   d. Two men recorded who walked with God:

     (1) Enoch (Gen. 5:22) — fellowship

     (2) Noah (Gen. 6:9) — faithfulness

e. These two elements make up friendship. In the Old Testament there was but one "friend of God," Abraham (Jas. 2:23; 2 Chron. 20:7); whereas in the New Testament all believers are called friends of Christ (John 15:13-15).

II. *The Secret of the Christian Life*

1. No enjoyment in relationship "except they be agreed."

2. "Meet by appointment" (R. V. marg.).

3. Same word used of Tabernacle in Wilderness, especially in connection with three of its main parts:

a. The Mercy Seat—"there I will meet with thee" (Exod. 25:22).

   (1.) Blood-stained ark typified Christ's sacrifice and propitiation for sin — God's presence there.

   (2.) We must meet Him at the Cross — or no Christian walk possible.

b. The Altar of Burnt Offering — "where I will meet you" (Exod. 29:42).

   (1.) Stood at door of Tabernacle and sacrifice was made every morning.

   (2.) Means entire consecration (Rom. 12:1) — or no Christian walk possible.

c. The Altar of Incense — "where I will meet with thee" (Exod. 30:36).

   (1.) Made a sweet scent daily.

   (2.) Typifies prayer and communion — or no Christian walk possible.

Thus, the word "agreed" has to do with
a. Conciliation.
b. Consecration.
c. Communion.

Conclusion

1. Will you "make an appointment" now?
    a. No special place, but with a special Person, in a special way, and at a special time.
    b. The Person is Christ; the way is faith; and the time is NOW.

2. Will you then keep the appointment constantly?
    a. Christ all along the way; faith always strong.
    b. Act leads to Attitude and then to Action.
    c. Conciliation (mercy-seat); consecration (burnt offering); communion (incense).
    d. Finally — "they shall walk with Me in white" (Rev. 3:4).

> Then all is peace and light
> This soul within;
> Then shall I walk with Thee,
> The loved Unseen;
> Leaning on Thee, my God,
> Guided along the road
>   Nothing between!

89

26.

Three Blessings

Obadiah 17 — "*Upon mount Zion shall be deliverance, and there shall be holiness: and the house of Jacob shall possess their possessions.*"

THE promises made to Israel concerning temporal blessings may be applied spiritually to the Church. Here is a prophecy of restoration and glory for Zion after bondage to the enemy Edom. It contains three promises; rescue from captivity, re-consecration to God, and recovery of former possessions; or, deliverance, holiness and enjoyment. These three sum up the blessings of Christianity and include all that God has for us.

I. *Safety* — "Upon Mount Zion be deliverance"

    1. From sin's condemnation (Rom. 8:1).

    2. From sin's power — in Satan (Acts 26:18; Heb. 2:14), in circumstances (Gal. 1:4), in self (Rom. 8:2) — or, "the world, the flesh and the devil."

    3. From sin's presence (Rev. 21:27).

II. *Sanctity* — "There shall be holiness"

    1. Set apart for God — consecration (Rom. 12:1).

    2. Filled with the Spirit of God — transformation (Rom. 12:2).

This also is a free gift, not an attainment; it is not "justification by faith" and "sanctification by fighting."

III. *Sufficiency* — "The house of Jacob shall posses their possessions."

The sons of the transformed "supplanter" shall now own and enjoy. We are Jacob's children in a spiritual sense.

1. All things come freely with the gift of Christ (Rom. 8:32; I Cor. 3:21, 22; I Tim. 6:17; II Peter 1:3). Therefore, possessing Christ is like owning an estate with infinite possibilites: e.g., wealth to be explored, soil to be cultivated, beauties to be enjoyed, and produce to be used. Cf. continent of Africa where settlements first hugged coast, leaving interior with all its wealth untapped.

2. After we are accepted in Christ, we are endowed in Him.

3. Our threefold title:
   a. God's purpose — "all your need" (Phil. 4:19).
   b. Christ's purchase — "purchased possession" (Eph. 1:14).
   c. The Spirit's power—"strengthened with might" (Eph. 3:16).

Conclusion

1. *The Possibility* — to have and yet not enjoy, because of ignorance, slothfulness, timidity, or contentment with less than best. We often have pailful when we might have ocean. Cf. Joshua 1:3, "every place," with I Kings 22:3, "take it not."

2. *The Purpose* — God's purpose for us is enjoyment through —

   a. Knowledge, which develops and increases (I Cor. 2:12).

   b. Faith, which accepts and claims (Mark 11:23, 24).

   c. Faithfulness, which appropriates and uses (I Tim. 6:17-19).

Examples of our possessions often unpossessed: inward peace, upward communication, outward victory. Let us follow a good example and "return unto the land of 'our' possession, and enjoy it" (Joshua 1:15), and even when, like Joshua, we are "old and stricken in years," there will remain "yet very much land to be possessed for "all things" are ours and we "are Christ's and Christ is God's" (I Cor. 3:21-23).

27

The Possibility of Failure

MARK 14:23, 31, 50—*"They all drank of it."*
"Likewise also said they all."
"They all forsook Him and fled."

IT is possible to stand on the bank of a stream which is so quiet that for a moment one hardly can tell in which direction the current is moving, or whether, indeed, there is a current at all. But as the eye sweeps the expanse of water it catches sight of a stake or a small tree which is strong enough to resist, and one soon sees the direction in which the stream is flowing.

Life is often like that placid stream: weeks and months and even years may flow by with not a ripple of sorrow or trouble or anxiety — nothing to show the direction of the life. But, sooner or later, some difficulty or bereavement or trial comes to test reality and power, and the true character of the life is revealed.

The disciples of Christ had spent three years with Jesus which were fairly quiet even though full of interest, enjoyment and inspiration. In His presence all was well, the flow of life steady even though the stream was not entirely clear. But then came a testing time and it revealed the trend of the disciple's lives by their weakness and their fall. This whole narrative is valuable because we are only what we are in an emergency. A crisis tests and special events show what use we have made of opportunities to store strength and build character. Above all, they reveal the genuineness of our Christian profession and whether we are truly born again.

I. *Fellowship Enjoyed* — "They all drank of it" (v. 23).

    1. *Sacred Privilege of True Friendship*

        a. In Orient, eating together had special significance — beggar, acquaintance, friend.

        b. Disciples had had three years of journeying and eating with Jesus—knowledge, love, friendship.

        c. This particular Passover meal had been according to the "desire" of Jesus (Luke 22:15).

    2. *Solemn Occasion of Loving Farewell*

        a. "Before I suffer" (Luke 22:15) — Jesus gradually leading up to revelation of death which had not hitherto been clear.

        b. Now come His words about "remembrance" of Him — a keepsake — a last word or look.

    3. *Significant Symbol of Great Salvation*

        a. During past years, words recorded in John 6 had foreshadowed Christ's death; now there is symbol, the "New Covenant."

        b. Atonement — sacrifice for sin of whole world.

THE POSSIBILITY OF FAILURE

II. *Faithfulness Assured* — "Likewise so said they all" (v. 31).

    1. *Sincere Expression of Loyal Gratitude.*

        a. Disciples' spirits uplifted — new privileges in sacrament — heard wondrous words recorded in John 14 — hearts glowed.

        b. Thrilled by loyalty and gratitude to Master — cheered by words recorded in John 15.

    2. *Strong Assertion of Real Constancy.*

        a. Not loud self-assertion but solemn vow and genuine love.

        b. Felt it incredible to fail such a Master.

    3. *Serious Ignorance of Personal Weakness.*

        a. Surprising self-confidence — almost boastful.

        b. Already forgot scattered sheep at smiting of shepherd, just quoted by Christ (v. 27) from Zechariah 13:7.

III. *Failure Manifested* — "They all forsook Him and fled" (v. 50).

    1. *Selfish Ingratitude after Continual Blessing*

        a. Cf. Christ's thought for them — "Come apart" (Mark 6:31) — "I have prayed" (Luke 22:32).

        b. Now He needed sympathy, but they fled, leaving Him alone and forgotten.

    2. *Sad Cowardice after Careful Training*

        a. Cf. teaching in John 16:33—"I have overcome" — and in Luke 10:19—"I give unto you power."

95

b. Even assurance about twelve legions of angels did not inspire their confidence. They thought all was lost.

3. *Surprising Unbelief after Close Relationship*

a. Secret, temporary loss of faith in Christ as Messiah.

b. Faith not completely eclipsed, after miracles; but sufficiently so to leave Christ solitary in His hour of suffering.

Conclusion

1. *A Great Privilege — Fellowship* (v. 23)

a. Fellowship means friends with nothing between (I John 1:7).

b. Christ our Peace has abolished enmity (Eph. 2:15).

c. The Lord's Supper beautiful expression of fellowship.

d. Christ *for* — atonement.
Christ *in* — life.
Christ *among* — fellowship.

2. *A Great Responsibility — Faithfulness* (v. 31).

a. Privilege implies responsibility.

b. Responsibility — our response to God's ability.

c. Danger in religious experience — dependence on emotion. Mr. Fact must lead Mr. Faith and only then comes Mr. Feeling (C. G. Trumbull).

d. Watchful — prayerful — trustful.

3. *A Great Disaster — Failure* (v. 50).

   a. Needless, unwarranted, unjustifiable.

   b. All that was needed was response.

   c. Yielding to Christ: submit, admit, commit, permit, transmit.

   d. Even after failure, we are to come back and make complete surrender, develop constant dependence, yield careful obedience.

So Christ will be all in all.

28.

Simeon

LUKE 2:25 (*R.V.*)—"*This man was righteous and devout, looking for the consolation of Israel: and the Holy Spirit was upon him.*"

THERE are few more interesting subjects for study than the group of choice souls associated with our Lord's birth and early days – Zachariah, Elizabeth, Mary, Joseph, Simeon, Anna. Of each something commendatory and distinctive is said, indicating the reality of his or her life and relation to God. Here Simeon illustrates the marks of the true Christian experience.

I. *The Elements of a True Life.*

    1. *In relation to the past* – "righteous"

        a. Sin forgiven and covered.

        b. Guilt removed for ever.

        c. Acceptance with God assured.

    2. *In relation to the present* – "devout"

        a. The saved sinner as a worshipper.

        b. A true attitude to an almighty, gracious God.

        c. Dependence – Delight – Demonstration.

3. *In relation to the future* — "looking for the consolation of Israel"

    a. The forward look of hope.

    b. Not to death but to Christ's coming (v. 26) — so we to His Second Advent.

    c. To look forward thus was "consolation," not dread — so we now.

II. *The Secret of a True Life* — "the Holy Spirit was upon him"

    1. The Spirit brings the soul to Christ (v. 27) who is our salvation (v. 30), and applies His righteousness (1 Tim. 3:16).

    2. The Spirit makes us truly devout and inspires our devotion (v. 28), sonship (Gal. 4:6), and holiness (2 Thess. 2:13).

    3. The Spirit inspires our hope by glorifying Christ (v. 32) and bringing His words to our remembrance (John 14:26).

Therefore all is by the Holy Spirit, in Him, and through Him.

Conclusion

The True Christian Life

    1. Means of its commencement — faith.

    2. Secret of its retention — love.

    3. Anticipation of its fulfilment — hope.

The Holy Spirit

1. Rests on the soul in conversion.

2. Reveals to the mind in consecration.

3. Replenishes the life in anticipation.

29.

Two Signs of Discipleship

LUKE 22:56, 58—*"This man was also with Him. . . . Thou art also of them."*

THOSE in the High Priest's house recognized Peter by two circumstances: he had been in the company of Jesus, and he had been in the company of Jesus' followers. These two marks on a person's life have always been indications of discipleship, and are the same today. A Christian is one who is united both to Christ and to other Christians. Hence we have a sure but simple test of a true Christian life.

I. *With Christ* — "with Him" (v. 56)

   1. *Salvation*
     Our great need in the past.

   2. *Sanctification*
     Our great need in the present.

   3. *Satisfaction*
     Our great need for past, present and future.
   All are found only in Christ.

II. *With Christians* — "of them" (v. 58)

   1. Oneness of life — in Christ.
       The Spirit animating.

2. Oneness of Love — to Christ
   The Spirit inspiring.

3. Oneness of Labor — for Christ
   The Spirit directing.

The New Testament connects the ideas of a church and fellowship. Cf. 1 John 1:3, 6, 7.

Conclusion

1. *Two simple tests.*
   a. What is Christ to me?
   b. What are my fellow-Christians to me?

   If I am not in their company, I must take heed and examine myself.

2. *Two simple secrets.*
   a. Abiding in Christ (1 John 2:5, 6).
   b. Love to others (1 John 2:10; 3:10).

30.

Andrew

JOHN 1:37, 40—*"The two disciples heard him (John) speak, and they followed Jesus. . . . One of the two was Andrew, Simon Peter's brother."*

THE Christian year really begins, not with the First Sunday in Advent but with St. Andrew's Day, November 30th. This emphasizes the factor of choice in the Christian life — Andrew "heard" and "followed" — and it is most appropriate, for he was one of the two very first Christians. In fact, the Christian Church actually began when these two followed Jesus. Hence, Andrew's may be called a typical life, a model for all those who belong to the Church of Christ. His very name suggests a typical man and reminds us of the great possibilities there are in manhood in and for Christ. We may trace a progressive revelation in the soul of Andrew.

I. *His Definite Conversion* (John 1:37)

1. *How?*
   He "heard" — simple Gospel sermon — the kind of preaching that always brings results.

2. *What?*
   He heeded — "followed Jesus" — willing trust and instant obedience.

103

II. *His Early Discipleship* (John 1:38, 39)

   1. *The Questions* (v. 38)

      a. Andrew had followed without a word — now Jesus asks direct question which the two men answer with another.

      b. They asked to know more of Jesus — a sure test of reality.

   2. *The Invitation* (v. 39)

      a. "Come and see" — They "came," they "saw," they "abode" — or we might paraphrase: They came, they saw, and Christ conquered. Abiding in Christ brings victory.

      b. They were indeed "practising the presence of Christ." Result seen next day in enthusiastic declaration based on experience.

III. *His Prompt Service* (John 1:41, 42)

   1. *Work soon followed.*

      a. Probably went home — where greatest test may be.

      b. Found brother — those nearest are often most difficult.

   2. *Method was wise.*

      a. "Brought" — not argued. Andrew let his brother Peter know that he himself had come to Jesus.

      b. Andrew not great man — but brought a great man.

IV. *His Full Consecration* (Matt. 4:18-20)

1. *The higher call.*
Faithfulness brought full responsibility of discipleship, leading in time to apostleship (Acts 1:15, 25, 26). Definitions: Disciple, one who accepts and follows; Apostle, a zealous advocate.

2. *The real meaning.*
All for Christ — now and always, at home or abroad.

V. *His Growing Experience* (John 6:8, 9)

1. *The great need* — the crowd — the disciples — the lad.

2. *The great secret* — Divine power through small means rightly used. Cf. Moses' rod, ram's horn, Gideon's fleece, widow's cruse of oil.

VI. *His Inquiring Mind* (Mark 13:3, 4)

Asked Christ questions about Second Coming — desire for more and deeper truth, and interest in "that blessed hope."

VII. *His Spiritual Perception* (John 12:20-23)

Strange visitors — something new — outside Israel. Philip turns to Andrew as though to say, "He will know what to do!" Andrew took the larger view, perhaps remembering what Christ had said about His "other sheep" (John 10:16).

Conclusion

We may sum up in two ways:

1. Conversion — Commission — Confirmation — Consecration — Communion.

2. Experience — Enquiry — Enthusiasm — Equipment — Evangelism.

All are vital — any omission loss of essential element in Christian life.

Each of us should either (a) go — himself; (b) let go — his children; (c) help go — his means. Illustrations: Seven Moravian brothers were all missionaries in Greenland, and all died. Their mother said that if there were seven more they should all go. Cutting pansies might be said to be robbing plants. No, for every one cut today there will be three new ones tomorrow; otherwise, the plants will go to seed. So Christianity gives and grows.

Faithfulness — Cf. Matthew 25:21; 1 Timothy 1:12; Revelation 2:10.

31.

Joy

Acts 13:52—"*The disciples were filled with joy, and with the Holy Ghost.*"

IF one should ask what one thing characterized the Christians of the New Testament, the answer would be, their joy. Among the chapters of the Book of Acts in which this characteristic attitude is seen are 2, 3, 4, 7, 8, 13 and 16. Is this true of Christians today? Is joy one of the marks distinguishing them from the people of the world? It may be argued that life is different now; but is it any less bright or easy? Is it not rather, in many ways, more so? The abolition of slavery from so much of the world is only one example of the amelioration of conditions in the old order which were not conducive to joy, and the very presence of Christianity and its undeniable influence on life is another instance. The fact is that joy is like the peace of God — the world can neither give it nor take it away.

I. *Joy — What It Means*

1. Joy is a condition, a state of soul due to being right with God.

2. Joy is not happiness.

107

     a. Happiness is dependent on happy circumstances, on what happens; joy is independent of these.

     b. Happiness depends on what one has; joy on what one is.

     c. Happiness comes from experience of good as distinct from evil; joy from experience of God apart from good or evil.

     d. Happiness comes from things outside which stir feelings within; joy leaps from within, from God in the heart and soul.

  3. Joy has three elements:

     a. Retrospection on revelation — faith — past.

     b. Aspiration after realization — love — present.

     c. Preparation in anticipation — hope — future.

II. *Joy — For Whom It Is*

For "the disciples" —

  1. Those who belong to Christ — not the world.

  2. All those who belong to Christ — not favored few only — all are "called to be saints."

III. *Joy — What It Does*

  1. It fortifies — mind and will.

  2. It satisfies — soul and heart.

Cf. Ethiopian eunuch (Acts 8:26-40) who "went on his way rejoicing" even though but a new convert with scanty knowledge, bereft of teacher, absolutely alone.

IV. *Joy — How It Comes*

With "the Holy Ghost" — incoming, indwelling. The "fulness of the Spirit" enters the yielded life, empty of self and world, and brings the "joy of the Lord."

Conclusion

Admit the Holy Spirit.
Permit Him to reveal Christ.
Commit to Him the life.
Transmit the resultant joy to others.

32.

The Manhood of the Son of God

JOHN 5:19, 20—"*The Son can do nothing of himself, but what he seeth the Father do; for what things soever he doeth, these also doeth the Son likewise. For the Father loveth the Son, and sheweth him all things that himself doeth: and he will shew him greater works than these, that ye may marvel.*"

EVERY fact in the human life of Christ is to be a factor in ours — such as His purity, His power, His peacefulness, His pattern, His prospect. It is interesting and helpful to read the Gospels with the thought of discovering their teaching concerning the character of Jesus. We find Him taking the position of a man, living moment by moment through the Holy Spirit sent down from the Father. We are apt to forget His perfect Manhood in our effort to keep always in view His Pre-eminent Godhood and to defend it. Yet each is essential, and though it is difficult, perhaps impossible, to reconcile the two, or even always to distinguish between them, we must accept both.

John's Gospel is the fullest expression of this perfect Manhood of Christ. In these verses of the fifth chapter we shall find four great principles of His life, and also His relationship to His Father and a corresponding relation between Christ and the believer.

I. *Entire Dependence*
1. *The Position* — "The Son"
    a. Life received — by Christ (John 5:26) — by the believer (John 1:12, 13).
    b. Life sustained — by Christ and by the believer (John 6:57).
2. *The Limitations* — "can do nothing of himself"
    a. He is the Channel, not the Source (John 5:30; 6:38).
    b. He is the Instrument and the Agent (John 4:34); so is the believer (John 15:5).
    Identity of sympathy, will and action — therefore of life itself.

II. *Constant Obedience*
1. *Watching* — "but what he seeth the Father do"
    a. Contemplating, learning, admiring, loving.
    b. The Work done — the Worker doing it.
2. *Imitating* — "these also doeth the Son likewise"
    a. The Matter — work for good of man and glory of God.
    b. The Manner — perfectly in character — appropriately for object.

III. *Blessed Intimacy*
1. *Loving* — "the Father loveth the Son"
    Interest and affection.
2. *Revealing* — "sheweth him all things that himself doeth"
    a. Privilege of intimacy — love has no secrets. Cf. Psalm 25:14; John 13:23-26.

  b. Extent of intimacy — "all things" — need of open mind and heart to receive. Cf. Epignosis of Paul's Epistles, e.g., 1 Cor. 13:12.

IV. *Growing Experience*

 1. *The Promise* — "he will shew him greater works than these" — Cf. miracle in John 5:1-16 with verse 21 — "quickeneth" (see chap. 11) and verse 22 — "judgment" (distant future).

 2. *The Purpose* — "that ye may marvel"
  "Strange things" (Luke 5:26) seen may result in faith by world or may not; but marveling also follows faith, so we may take it to ourselves as we watch the Lord's working.

Conclusion

 Blessed intimacy and growing experience are only possible when entire dependence and constant obedience characterize the life. All are necessary to a full, effective Christian testimony. Are we following our Lord's perfect example?

33

The Two Comforters

JOHN 14:16—*"I will pray the Father, and he shall give you another Comforter, that He may abide with you forever."*

ONE has only to observe the size of a crowd watching the progress of a building on some city street to realize the interest that such an operation — its commencement, development, and completion — has for the average man. The foundation of the structure must be deep, and broad, and strong; and its walls and its roof must be solid, and firm, and lasting.

Through each succeeding Church year, the members of the Church are called upon to consider the history of her building. The Incarnate Word is her foundation — deep with the mystery of God, broad enough to reach all, and solid with Divine strength. The Church's walls may be identified with Christ's Life, His Death, His Resurrection, and His Ascension — all of which are solid in material, firm in execution, and lasting in nature; and these lead up to the "roof" or climax of the structure, the descent of the Holy Spirit of God.

All of Christ's life prior to the Cross, although perfect, was preliminary in the sense of His own frequent statements (e.g., John 7:39; 12:32; 14:12, 26, 28, 29; 15:26, 27; 16:7-28). The word used by Him to describe the Holy

Spirit is translated into English as "Comforter." This term, however, is too narrow to cover the whole significance of the Greek word that is transliterated "Paraclete," "one called in to help." The Holy Spirit *is* a Consoler, but He is far more. Perhaps the very best modern term would be "Representative" — one who takes charge of a matter for someone and sees it through; for the Holy Spirit is God's Representative in the life of the believer and of the Church as a whole.

This reminds us of the word "Advocate," used of our Lord in 1 John 2:1. It is indeed the same word, "paracletos"; so that we are not surprised to read in our text the promise, "He (the Father) shall give you *another Comforter.*" Yes, there are two Comforters, or Advocates, or Representatives — Jesus Christ, and the Holy Spirit. Further, the word for "another" does not connote one who is *instead of* someone else, but rather, a second person who is *in addition to* a first. Neither does it suggest another of a different kind (eteros), but rather, another of the same kind (allos). For a passage where two Greek words translated "another" appear in contrast, see Galatians 1:6-9: "A different gospel which is in no sense an addition to the true one" might be the literal rendering. In brief, then, the Holy Spirit is an additional Comforter of the same kind as Christ, which is consistent wth the essential oneness of the Holy Trinity.

Note their relation to each other and to the believer:

I. *Jesus Christ is our Representative with the Father.* He was the Paraclete "called in" by the Father to obtain our salvation. Christ with the Father is the guarantee for us of

1. *Forgiveness* — the past pardoned.

    a. High Priest celebrated Day of Atonement outside, then passed through to Holy of Holies.

114

So Christ ascended into heaven "now to appear in the presence of God for us" (Heb. 9:24).

b. There He guarantees acceptance of sacrifice of Himself, and man is at peace with God.

c. Said He would offer Himself — "gave Himself a ransom for many" (Mark 10:45) and did (1 Tim. 2:6).

d. Man could never have entered heaven if Christ's ransom had not been accepted. So Christ in heaven guarantees pardon for sin.

2. *Grace* — the present supplied.

a. High Priest had to return after sacrifice, which was impermanent because sin was recurrent; so Day of Atonement took place annually.

b. Christ's sacrifice was "once for all" (Heb. 10:10).

c. Because He lives — just as He lives — as long as He lives — we "shall live also" (John 14:19) — "after the power of an endless life" (Heb. 7:16). So Christ in heaven guarantees grace for living.

3. *Glory* — the future revealed.

a. High Priest's mediations all speak of past and present. Future "was not yet made manifest" (Heb. 9:8).

b. So Christian's past and present obviously supplied, but what about future — e.g., longings, loved ones, questionings?

c. Christ answers all questions. He was our "Fore-runner" (Heb. 6:20) "within the veil" (Heb. 6:19) — which figure denotes that others come after. He is our Firstfruits (1 Cor. 16:20, 23), the pledge of our own ascension into glory.

Thus Jesus Christ, representing us to the Father, obtains for us forgiveness, grace, and glory. But all of this would be merely objective, outside realities for us, rather than possessions to be obtained and appropriated by us, were it not that

II. *The Holy Spirit is Christ's Representative in Us*
He is the Paraclete "called in" by Christ to bestow the salvation obtained by Christ. The Holy Spirit in us guarantees what Christ did, makes it ours, and makes Christ real in our lives.

1. *Acceptance* — forgiveness assured

   a. Gospel heard — need felt — conditions, faith and surrender, fulfilled.

   b. Then Holy Spirit "beareth witness with our spirit" (Rom. 8:16). Cf. Gal. 4:6; 1 John 5:6.

   c. Then come consciousness of forgiveness and restoration to Divine favor.

2. *Life* — grace given

   a. When Divine life is born it abides — is an indwelling Presence — adheres and inheres.

   b. Holy Spirit makes Christ real, makes Him to us what He was to disciples, and more, for presence is internal and permanent — "strengthened with might by His Spirit in the inner man that Christ may dwell in your hearts by faith" (Eph. 3:16, 17).

c. Life — growth — power — obedience — comfort —— all! (Cf. Gal. 2:20)

3. *Hope* — glory begun

a. Soul looks on to future as well as back to past and around on present. "Hope springs eternal in the human breast" (Wordsworth).

b. Holy Spirit points way. Cf. 1 Cor. 2:9; 2 Cor. 1:22; Eph. 1:13, 14; 4:30; Col. 1:27.

c. Sweet fellowship assured continuously, permanently, eternally.

Thus the Holy Spirit, representing Christ to us, bestows forgiveness, grace, and glory obtained by Christ in His death. Objective facts become subjective possessions; outward revelations become inward experiences.

Conclusion

So two Comforters — and both necessary. We may tabulate as follows:

Christ in Heaven	*The Holy Spirit on Earth*
Linking us to God	Uniting us to Christ
Representing us to God	Representing Christ to us
Presenting our prayers to God	Inspiring our Prayers to God
Is our Way to God	Leads us along the way of life
Reveals God as Father	Reveals Christ as Lord
Personifies the Truth of God	Points to Christ as Truth
Has completed the work of salvation	Instils trust in the work of Christ

Has laid the foundation of the Church	Builds us upon the Foundation which is Christ
Is preparing a place for us	Is preparing us for that place

"Come, Holy Spirit, come,
Let Thy bright beams arise,
Dispel the sorrow from our minds,
The darkness from our eyes.

"Convince us all of sin,
Then guide to Jesus' blood;
And to our wondering view reveal
The secret love of God.

"Cheer our desponding hearts,
Thou heavenly Paraclete,
Give us to lie with humble hope
At our Redeemer's feet.

" 'Tis Thine to cleanse the heart,
To sanctify the soul,
To pour fresh life in every part
And new create the whole."

34.

The Christian's Stronghold

JOHN 14:20—*"At that day ye shall know I am in my Father, and ye in me, and I in you."*

A PIECE of ordinary glass has only one surface; it is seen in its entirety at one glance. Crystal, on the other hand, has several surfaces or facets, each complete in itself and yet connected with one another and combining to make a beautiful, harmonious whole. God's truth is like crystal rather than glass. It is a whole and yet many-sided, each facet complete in itself and yet proportioned and necessary to the whole. It is a temptation to emphasize one element in Christian truth to the exclusion of others, but this is something to be avoided. The fact is that truth is of most value when viewed as a whole with all elements combined. Human, Divine — philosophical, practical — each must be given its proper place. Each age emphasizes a different facet of truth: Nicaea, Reformation, our own day. At the Council of Nicaea, for instance, the Godhead of Christ, His Life and Death were all given precedence; in the Reformation, the doctrine of the free, direct access of the believer to God was emphasized; and of late, we may say, the doctrine of the indwelling presence of the Holy Spirit is one which has been given special emphasis.

I. *Our Safe Protection* — "I in my Father"

  1. *The Meaning* — Christ's Authority

    a. To Teach

      (1) Claimed to come from Father.

      (2) Claimed to reveal Father.

      (3) Yet was opposed and rejected — His veracity at stake.

    b. To Save

      (1) Cf. Luke 19:10; John 2:19; 12:32.

      (2) Miracles to substantiate — Gr. "signs."

      (3) Yet ascribed to Beelzebub — awful alternative.

  2. *The Knowledge* — Christ's Authority Acknowledged

    "At that day ye shall know . . ." How?

    a. The Resurrection

      (1) The Father's acknowledgment (Rom. 1:4).

      (2) Christ's own power and position.

      (3) "Many infallible proofs" (Acts 1:3).

    b. The Holy Spirit

      (1) Christ had promised — promise fulfilled at Pentecost.

      (2) By fruits — Cf. world since with world before.

Therefore, our Safe Protection — the Godhead of Jesus Christ.

II. *Our Strong Position* — "ye in me"

1. *The Meaning* — Acceptance
   a. Christ's Pardon

      (1) Sin under punishment — consciousness of wrong. How to be rid of guilt?

      (2) "Canst thou not minister to a mind diseased?" — the world's plea.

      (3) Christ's remedy — in "Me" — identification with Him.

   b. Christ's Righteousness

      (1) Sin separates — makes character unholy. How shall men have access to God?

      (2) Christ's offer — robe on man — Spirit in him.

      (3) "Jehovah Tsidkenu" — "In the Lord, righteousness" — we draw near in Christ.

2. *The Knowledge* — Assurance

   a. Christ's Death

      (1) Paid penalty — Cf. Isa. 53:4-6; Rom. 4:25.

      (2) Made atonement — Resurrection proved acceptance.

      (3) Purchased pardon — Cf. Eph. 1:6

    b. Christ's Life

       (1) The Sinless One made sin (2 Cor. 5:21)

       (2) Righteousness reckoned and bestowed.

       (3) Resurrection and ascension in proof.

Therefore, our Strong Position — to be in Christ.

III. *Our Sure Provision* — "I in you"

   1. *The Meaning* — Ability

    a. Life

      (1) Our need not only pardon but power — moment by moment, in the Spirit.

      (2) Character and conduct involved.

      (3) Christ's claim — "I am come" (John 5:43; 10:10) — "I am the Life" (John 14:6).

    b. Hope

      (1) Anticipation of future — longings and yearnings.

      (2) Future life — dear ones gone on before.

      (3) Christ's claim — "In you the hope of glory" (Col. 1:27).

   2. *The Knowledge* — Assurance

    a. Inward Witness

      (1) Christ in believer — Cf. Gal. 2:20.

      (2) Peace brings assurance.

    b. Outward Proof

      (1) Conduct — Cf. John 14:15; 1 John 3:14.

      (2) Fruit — Cf. Gal. 5:22-26 — power over sin.

Therefore, our Sure Provision is to have Christ in us.

IV. *Our Satisfying Privilege* — "ye shall know"

  1. How?

    a. By experience.

    b. By verifying faculty of mind.

    c. By witness of heart, conscience, and will.

    d. By faith and not by sight.

  2. When? — "in that day"

    a. Christ has been, is, much — but will be all in all.

    b. More known of

      (1) Father's loving sympathy and melting tenderness;

      (2) Saviour's full pardon and free righteousness.

      (c) Spirit's enabling and inspiring.

    c. Earth's day done? Hardly dawned!

Conclusion

Thus "be ye also ready" for "eye hath not seen" and "God shall wipe away all tears."

> "His knowledge, His love and His care
> For our safety and guidance are given,
> That here we may taste of His peace
> And thus share the joy of His Heaven."

35.

"Life" in St. John's Gospel

JOHN 20:31—*"These were written . . . that believing ye might have life through his name."*

NATURE speaks with one voice — the voice of Life. Life is also the deepest, fullest manifestation of Christianity, and, conversely, Christianity is the deepest, fullest manifestation of life. It is a justification and a fulfilment of life, and, like life itself, is a gift of God to man.

In the New Testament there are many phrases which include the word "life." To quote only a few of these, we are told to "walk in newness of life" (Rom. 6:4) ; the Holy Spirit is called "the Spirit of life" (Rom. 8:2) ; and Christ is said to have been made a Priest "after the power of an endless life" (Heb. 7:16). Perhaps this emphasis on life is pre-eminently true of St. John's Gospel, as indicated by our text, which is part of the Book's conclusion or summing-up. We may therefore trace this principle of Divine Life step by step through the Gospel.

1. *The Source of Life* (1:4)

   1. The fount and starting-point — "in him was life."

   2. Man's light from God's life — "the life was the light of men."

II. *The Beginning of Life* (3:7)

1. The new birth — "ye must be born again."

2. The alternative — death: "perish" (3:15, 16); "shall not see life" (3:36).

III. *The Indwelling of Life* (4:14)

1. Reception followed by realization — "the water that I shall give him . . . everlasting life."

2. Salvation followed by satisfaction — "shall never thirst."

IV. *The Permanence of Life* (5:24)

1. Future as well as present and past.

   a. "*Shall not* come into condemnation."

   b. "*Hath* everlasting life."

   c. "*Hath passed* out of death into life" (R.V.).

2. Eternal in duration because eternal in quality.

V. *The Sustenance of Life* (6:27, 33, 51)

1. Physical life depends on absorption and assimilation of matter, making flesh and blood.

2. Spiritual life, similarly, is sustained by Christ, the Living Bread.

VI. *The Abundance of Life* (10:10)

1. Not merely life, but as much life as possible — "have it more abundantly."

2. Not content with less or a difference of degree of warmth.

3. A double blessing — a soul saved from sin, and a heart secured for service.

VII. *The Condition of Life* (11:25; 12:25)

    1. "The resurrection" comes before "the life." Our life is through the death and rising again of Christ.

    2. Relation between Christ's death and resurrection and ours (Cf. Rom. 6:10; 1 Cor. 15:22, 36; Eph. 2:1, 5).

VIII. *The Outcome of Life* (15:5, 6, 8)

    1. Abiding — a great word of St. John (Cf. 5:38; 14:16)

    2. Fruitfulness (Cf. Gal. 5:22, 23)

IX. *The Glory of Life* (17:2, 3)

    1. The means of eternal life — power of Christ (v. 2).

    2. The essence of eternal life — knowledge of God (v. 3).

Conclusion

Two classes of people: "quick" and "dead" — alive and asleep. Which are we?

> "The spring of the life that is flowing
>> Is hidden with Christ in God;
> Not yet the mystery knowing,
> I feel that the peace is growing,
>> As a river grows deep and broad."

36.

Manifold Grace

John 21:7, 8—*"That disciple whom Jesus loved saith unto Peter, It is the Lord. Now when Simon Peter heard that it was the Lord, he . . . cast himself into the sea. And the other disciples came in a little ship."*

In his First Epistle, St. Peter writes of "the manifold grace of God." One wonders if, in using this phrase, he may have had in mind the scene of our text. God's grace is many-sided and is intended for numberless types of people. These may be exemplified by the persons mentioned in these verses. Man is apt to limit his experience to well-worn grooves, so it is essential to keep in mind the infinite variety of God's dealings.

Jesus Christ works on and through the differing temperaments of men, and thus, in this scene on the shore of Galilee, He showed Himself in different ways. He watched over these fishermen followers of His, He spoke to them, He fed them, and all were loved by Him and all were disciples of His; but their after life and ministry varied with their differing temperaments. Jesus is on the shore of our life and it is ours to respond to Him, even though in varying ways. There was

I. *Clear Insight* — John

   1. Love, the great perceptive power.

      a. All through, John was near to Christ and perhaps knew His deepest secrets.

      b. To love at all we must know — head before heart.

      c. Then, to fully know we must love — heart before head.

   2. Love, the great penetrating power.

      a. Sees God in everything. Cf. Christ here in relation to daily toil and disappointment.

      b. Ignores second causes — logic thrown to winds — "It is the Lord!"

II. *Eager Enthusiasm* — Peter

   1. Less capacity for delicate sensibility.

      a. Not much insight.

      b. Dependence on another for that.

   2. Lion's boldness, if not eagle's eye.

      a. Burning enthusiasm — not piercing vision.

      b. No calculation of consequences.

   3. But also manifestation of love.

      a. Fervency — impulsiveness — strong affection based on gratitude and admiration.

      b. We need both John and Peter.

III. *Ordinary Service* — the other disciples

1. As important because necessary to work.
   a. Not see, nor swim, but row!
   b. Knowledge of craft — practical ability.
   c. No prophet's eye, no enthusiast's heart — yet love and practical devotion.

2. As sincere even though not so showy.
   a. Cf. Martha and Mary (John 11) : it was Martha, the practical, who "went" while Mary, the spiritual, "sat" (v. 20) ; Martha who said not only "if" but also "but," Mary who said only "if" and wept hopelessly (vs. 22, 23, 32, 33) ; Martha only who said, "I believe" (v. 27) .
   b. Thus, the devotee and the enthusiast sometimes fail in crises, while others plod on in humble trust.
   c. Where would the Church be without such?

3. As noble, even though not so unusual.
   a. Ordinary drudgery may be transformed into ordination to serve (Acts 6) .
   b. Peter and John no more prompt than others in landing — "they" (v. 9) .

Conclusion

1. A gentle hint — careful in dealings with others — not depreciate — all needed. "Followeth not us" — who are *we?*

2. A precious encouragement — not all are outstanding — good thing, too. "They also serve who only stand and wait."

3. A necessary duty — to be balanced Christian — cultivate all possibilities:

   a. First type in danger of impracticality — so second.

   b. Second type in danger of rashness — so third.

   c. Third type in danger of secularity — so first and second.

4. A strong incentive

   a. Begin with third type — ordinary, faithful.

   b. Love grows by serving — thus first type.

   c. Obedience not only test but means of love — thus second type.

"By love serve one another."

> "And daily, hourly, loving and giving
> In the poorest life makes heavenly living."

37.

The Face of An Angel

Acts 6:15—*"All . . . saw his face as it had been the face of an angel."*

THIS is a remarkable description. How did Luke know what an angel looked like? Had he heard from Mary or Peter who had seen one, or was this an echo of Paul's eyewitness account in the light of later experience? In any event, Luke probably could give no truer description of Stephen's face, for an angel then, as now, suggests the highest ideal of character and appearance, although there is a sense in which a saved sinner in his glorified body will outshine the most resplendent of the angelic host and sing

> "A song which even angels
> Can never, never sing;
> They know not Christ as Saviour,
> But worship Him as King."

The face of any created being is highly indicative of character.

I. *What Characterizes the Face of an Angel?*

1. Light
   a. Cf. Matt. 28:3 — intelligence, moral excellence, glory.

b. Face should show (1) intelligence, and (2) sincerity.

c. Cf. Acts 6:3 and 10 — "wisdom."

2. Warmth

a. Cf. Acts 6:10 — "spirit" — attractiveness, lovingkindness.

b. Face with light but no warmth likely to be "icily regular, splendidly null."

3. Repose

a. Light only tends to over-anxious thought — warmth only to too great vivacity.

b. Balance of repose needed — no care or unrest.

4. Strength

a. Light, warmth, and repose only can be weak.

b. Strength needed to complete picture. Cf. Psa 103:20; Judg. 13:6.

These four elements of a noble face may also be called: Truth, Love, Peace, Power.

II. *Why Was Stephen's Face like that of an Angel?*

1. It was revealing — light

a. There is a revelation of heaven in a good face.

b. Cf. Exod. 34:29-35 with 2 Cor. 3:7, also Matt. 17:2 with Luke 9:29.

132

2. It was attractive — warmth

   a. Face and manner count in God's service, showing sympathy and kindliness, and inspiring trust.

   b. Others see (Exod. 34:30) even if the owner does not (v. 29).

3. It was glorifying — repose

   a. Peaceful face has air of glory.

   b. Reminds how beautiful God must be if His reflection is — cf. sun and moon.

4. It was reassuring — strength

   a. A strong face brings comfort.

   b. It spells an indefinable power — possible for all because it derives from character, not from position or possessions or intellect.

III. *What is the Secret of an Angelic Face?*

1. Privileged Position

   a. Angels see God (Matt. 18:10), and so did Stephen (Acts 7:55).

   b. Cf. 2 Cor. 3:18; 4:6 — shining in heart makes shining out of face.

   c. Cf. Heb. 2:9 with 12:2 — nearness begets likeness when heart is right.

2. *Personal Purity*

   a. Face index of nature and occupation (Luke 9:29).

   b. When off guard, character will out.

133

    c. "Pure in heart" denotes holiness of entire personality.

    d. We grow like those we love — so let us love God.

3. Perfect Obedience

    a. Disobedience darkens face.

    b. Greek word for "angel" means also "messenger."

    c. Obedience makes for a serene countenance, for whole being is in the full will of God.

4. Perpetual Fellowship

    a. Basis — abiding.

    b. Two sides to fellowship:

        (1) Human — faith, surrender, trust make avenues of being open;

        (2) Divine — bestowal of Holy Spirit makes avenues of being full.

Stephen experienced both of these.

> "Satisfied and full of favor
>   By my King I stand,
> Having blessings without number
>   From His opened hand;
> Oh, the richness of His treasure,
> Oh, the greatness of His measure,
> Oh, the fulness of my pleasure,
>   As His gifts expand!"

c. Cf. verse 5 — "a man full of faith and of the Holy Ghost."

Conclusion

The Duty of All
Rendering of due — debt of love.

2. The Privilege of All
To reflect God and attract others.

3. The Power of All
No comparable power on earth.

4. The Possibility of All
God is able and will shine through the surrendered personality.

Therefore, Think God's thoughts by meditation
Receive God's life by trust
Live in God's presence by prayer
Do God's will by obedience